W9-ARP-751

Library Media Center
N   Central School
Madison, N.Y., 13402

SAMUEL
GOLDWYN

Movie Mogul

SAMUEL
GOLDWYN

Movie Mogul

By

Jeremy Barnes

THE AMERICAN DREAM

SILVER BURDETT PRESS
ENGLEWOOD CLIFFS, NEW JERSEY

Text © 1989 by Silver Burdett Press

All rights reserved including the right of reproduction in whole or in part in any form. Published by Silver Burdett Press, a division of Simon & Schuster, Inc., Englewood Cliffs, New Jersey.

Designed and produced by Blackbirch Graphics, Inc.

Project Editor: Nancy Furstinger

Manufactured in the United States of America

(Lib. ed.) 10 9 8 7 6 5 4 3 2 1

(Paper ed.) 10 9 8 7 6 5 4 3 2 1

Library of Congress Cataloging-in-Publication Data

Barnes, Jeremy.
  Samuel Goldwyn.
    (The American dream)
  Bibliography: p.123
  Includes index.
  Summary: Discusses the career and films of the colorful and difficult personality, Sam Goldwyn, a motion picture producer for much of the twentieth century, who paid those who worked for him lavishly and insisted on high quality.
    1. Goldwyn, Samuel, 1882–1974—Juvenile literature.
2. Motion picture producers and directors—United States—Biography— Juvenile literature. [1. Goldwyn, Samuel, 1882–1974.   2. Motion picture producers and directors]
I. Title.   II. Series: American Dream (Englewood Cliffs, N.J.)
PN1998.3.G65B37   1988   791.43'0232'0924 [B] [92] 88-30564
ISBN 0-382-09586-3 (lib. bdg.)
ISBN 0-382-09594-4 (pbk.)

Contents

Before World War I, an average of 3,000 immigrants arrived at Ellis Island each day.

Chapter 1

Two Beginnings

*I*n September 1895, a Polish boy of thirteen disembarked from a ship into the crowded, echoing halls of the immigration center at Ellis Island, in New York harbor. He was one of the tens of thousands of European Jews, many of them from Russia and Poland, who immigrated to the United States in the late nineteenth century. They flocked to America dreaming of freedom and prosperity.

The boy, Samuel Goldfisch, was filled with that dream. He also was gifted with an unusual amount of drive and imagination. On his arrival in the United States, he assumed that whatever future he had lay in making gloves, the kind of small handwork business that many immigrants brought from the old country. He could not have imagined that his ultimate fortune and fame would be achieved in a field that was just then in the process of being invented, and that the entire world would come to know him not as Sam Goldfish, glovemaker, but as Samuel Goldwyn, motion-picture producer. In 1895 Sam had never heard of motion pictures. Neither had most Americans.

He traveled a long, circuitous route to his ultimate career. Samuel Goldfisch was born in the Jewish ghetto of Warsaw, Poland, on August 27, 1882. In the nineteenth century, Jews had migrated from small towns all over Poland to Warsaw, hoping to improve their lives and fortunes. The result had been very little improvement. In the narrow, dark streets of the ghetto, tens of thousands scratched out a poor living, mostly doing handwork in small shops. Moreover, Poland was part of the Russian empire, and Russia had enacted stringent anti-Semitic laws. Though Jews in Warsaw were not subject to the massacre that drove many Jews from Russia, they were still harassed and victimized by oppressive laws. In the late nineteenth century, Jews from all over Eastern Europe began a wave of immigration to England and to America, looking for a better life.

Sam arrived in New York with no money, virtually no schooling, and still speaking hardly a word of English.

Sam's parents, Abraham and Hannah Goldfisch (a clerk at Ellis Island would drop the *c*), pampered their firstborn son and gave him a lifelong expectation of being treated in this fashion. In his maturity, Samuel Goldwyn was evasive about his childhood; he seemed embarrassed about his beginnings in a poor Jewish ghetto. According to one story, his parents died, and then, at eleven, he ran away to the house of an aunt in Birmingham, England. At other times he spoke of visiting his mother in Europe.

In any event, in 1893 young Sam arrived in Birmingham, where he worked for nearly two years as a common laborer, pushing a cart, assisting a blacksmith, and doing other menial jobs. Surrounded by other immigrants from Eastern Europe, Sam spoke only Polish and Yiddish. In later years he would recall walking the streets with nothing on his mind but the next loaf of bread. As hard as things were, he still managed to save money for his real goal—the voyage to America, the land of opportunity. Eventually he accumulated enough for a steerage ticket across the Atlantic. It was not an easy journey, for the passengers in steerage, the cheapest class, were stowed in large holds like cattle. Sam arrived in New York with no money, virtually no schooling, and still speaking hardly a word of English.

Sam had already arranged to be apprenticed to relatives of some English friends. These relatives were glovemakers in Gloversville, New York, northwest of Albany. Rather than settling on New York's Lower East Side as many immigrants did, Sam set out across the state to Gloversville. For the next several years he would rise at six in the morning to walk to work at the factory, standing all day at a glovemaking machine.

He later admitted that he never showed much promise as a glovemaker. The work didn't interest him, and he had begun to get other ideas. Sam admired the traveling salesmen, called "drummers," who hung around the hotel in Gloversville. "How I envied them," he later said, "those splendid adventurers with their hats and their massive cigars both at an angle! For to me, they represented the everlasting romance of the far horizon."

With his usual energy and determination, Sam began taking an English course at night school after the long day's work. In a year of study he acquired a unique style of English. It was full of "malapropisms" and a strange logic, but it would serve him for the rest of his career. In 1902 he became an American citizen.

When he was sixteen, Sam began to pester his boss, Samuel Lehr, for a chance to be a salesman, like the drummers around the hotel. Lehr resisted at first, because of Sam's age and dubious English. Finally, Sam secured the job by agreeing to take on the sales territory where Lehr's business had always

At Ellis Island, each immigrant was required to take health and literacy tests. If they did not pass they could be refused entry.

been the worst—the Berkshire hills in western Massachusetts. Perhaps Lehr believed the experience would cure this teenager of his grand ambitions and send him running back to the factory. Arriving in Massachusetts, in new clothes and with a sample case in hand, Sam went to the biggest department store in Pittsfield, which had never bought a pair of gloves from Samuel Lehr. The buyer told the anxious young salesman that they still had no intention of ordering any.

Finally, in desperation, Sam laid his cards on the table: "I told him this was my chance and if I failed I was finished." Amazingly, the buyer took pity on the boy and placed a three-hundred-dollar order. Sam was in business, and he attacked his territory with a vengeance.

He became a master salesman, adept at persuading, pestering, backslapping, charming, wheedling, and all the other necessary skills of the profession. Coupled with these skills was a tireless energy. Soon he had turned Lehr's worst territory into one of the best. When Lehr had an opening for a salesman in New York City, the job went to Sam Goldfish.

A few years later Sam became sales manager for another glove company in New York City. Before long he was the highest-paid glove salesman in the country, a partner in the business, making about $15,000 a year—a fabulous income in an era when ten dollars a week was a good salary. Now he could indulge in expensive clothes and trips to Europe. It had been an astonishing rise for the young man—he had done what every immigrant dreamed of doing. The trouble was, as he said later, "although at thirty I was a comparatively successful man, I was not satisfied."

He began to dream of some new kind of business, something that was just getting started, where he could get in on the ground floor with no one ahead of him and where the opportunity to grow was unlimited. As it happened, a chain of coincidences was to lead him in exactly that direction.

Sam had developed a passion for the theater and especially for actors and actresses: "I used to fall in love every night, practically. And . . . I cried my eyes out [at the plays]." He developed a taste for ballet as well, and attended lectures to fill in the enormous gaps in his education. During this period, Sam became attracted to a bright-eyed young lady named Bessie Ginzberg, the niece of his boss in the glove company. Bessie, however, ignored Mr. Goldfish and married Jesse Lasky. Her husband had once been a vaudeville performer and was now a theatrical agent representing many people in vaudeville—the variety world of singers, comedians, animal acts, acrobats, and whatever else diverted an audience.

Goldfish and Lasky became friends. Sam was drawn to Lasky's house partly by his interest in the stage and partly by Jesse's sister Blanche, whom he had met shortly before. As a child, Blanche had played the cornet in a vaudeville act with her brother; now she ran Jesse's office efficiently. Blanche was ready for marriage, and Sam was drawn to the vivacious, attractive girl with a good head for business. They were married in 1910.

Sam and Blanche moved in with the Laskys, sharing a small apartment on Broadway. Jesse began to be bombarded regularly with Sam's ideas about finding an entirely new venture, something that would make a real fortune for them both. Lasky made various suggestions—including several mining projects and even a plan for selling tamales in California—which Sam impatiently rejected. At the same time, Sam became involved in Lasky's theater projects. Together they backed a Broadway comedy called *Cheer Up,* which was produced by a friend of Lasky's named Cecil B. DeMille. The play flopped, but soon something more promising came to the attention of Sam Goldfish.

In early 1911, Sam wandered for the first time into one of the seedy theaters called *nickelodeons,* which had sprung up over the previous five years around the city, mostly in the poor immigrant neighborhoods. These places featured the new invention called motion pictures.

Later, Samuel Goldwyn would recall the scene of that day—a player piano "digging viciously into a waltz," the floor covered with peanut shells, and in the darkness men, women, and children chewing gum or munching peanuts as the pictures flickered magically across the screen. The short films came one after another: cowboys on horseback galloped over the plains, the Three Musketeers dueled manfully, Carmen arrived at the fatal bullfight. The only sounds were the out-of-tune piano, the crunch of peanuts, the rattle of the projector, the murmurs and exclamations of the crowd. The films were crude, hackneyed in plot, scratched, and dim. But to Sam Goldfish, they were the most wonderful thing he had ever seen, the answer to all his dreams.

Chapter 2

Into the
Movies

Whithen Sam Goldfish saw his
first movies in 1911, the film industry in the United
States was at a low ebb. A dozen years before, movies
had been one of the great novelties of the age. Now
that the novelty had worn off, no one had managed
to make movies exciting enough as drama or spectacle to transform them into an art. In 1911, however,
the movies were on the brink of taking that step, and
with his usual luck, Sam was drawn into the business at exactly the right moment.

Motion pictures had not been invented all at
once; they developed through a series of discoveries
over many years. The ancient Greeks had been
aware of the physical phenomenon that is the basis of
motion pictures. Called persistence of vision, it
causes the human brain to retain a given image from
the eye for a fraction of a second before it absorbs the
next image. It is for that reason alone that still pic-

Right: *A 1912 advertisement for the Edison Kinetoscope includes a selection of films available from the Edison Company.*

Below: *Thomas Alva Edison (1847–1931) was the inventor of the typewriter, the record player, the incandescent electric lamp, and the kinetoscope.*

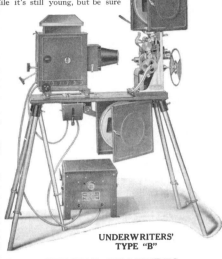

THE EDISON KINETOSCOPE

An Unsurpassed Moving Picture Machine from every point of view. "Once used, always used."

The motion picture show is fast becoming the biggest factor in the amusement field—the biggest money-maker for the men who are playing the game with both eyes open. Go into the business NOW, while it's still young, but be sure to START with the right machine. A cheap machine is a bad investment and a losing proposition from the beginning.

The Edison Kinetoscope projects the clearest, steadiest pictures, is the simplest machine to operate, is absolutely safe and will outwear any other motion picture machine made.

Write us today for a catalog and a copy of the Edison Kinetogram.

COMING EDISON FILMS

Tell your exchange you want them

May 10—7033. Treasure Island, by Robert Louis Stevenson. 1,050 feet. Drama.
May 11—7034. Every Rose Has Its Stem, by Ethel Browning. 1,000 feet. Comedy-drama.
May 14—7035. The Bank President's Son, by Marion Brooks. 1,000 feet. Drama.
May 15—7036. A Personal Affair. 1,000 feet. Comedy.
May 17—7038. The Convict's Parole, by Melvin G. Winstock. 1,000 feet. Dramatic.
May 18. 7039. A Romance of the Ice Fields. 635 feet. Dramatic.
7040. Scenes in Delhi, India. 365 feet. Descriptive.
May 21—7041. Their Hero, from " At Good Old Siwash," by George Fitch. 1,000 feet. Comedy.
May 22—7042. The Artist and the Brain Specialist, by Harry Furniss. 1,000 feet. Comedy-drama.
May 24—7043. The Sunset Gun, by Bannister Merwin. 1,000 feet. Dramatic.
May 25—7044. A Western Prince Charming, from " A Chaparral Prince," by O. Henry. 1,000 feet. Dramatic
May 28—7045. Jim's Wife. 1,000 feet. Dramatic.
May 29—7046. The Passion Flower. 1,000 feet. Comedy.
May 31—7047. Views in Calcutta. India. 1,000 feet. Descriptive.

Thomas A. Edison
INCORPORATED

267 Lakeside Ave., Orange, N. J.

UNDERWRITERS' TYPE "B"

SPECIAL FEATURES:

Adjustable Outside Revolving Shutter, Chain Take-Up, Extra Large House with square condenser holder, Double Magazine Rollers, Heavy Brass Terminals on connecting cords, set of Heavy Extension Legs, four of which are 1 1-4 inches in diameter. A very substantial stand.

Price, with Rheostat, 110 volt, 25-40 amperes, - $225.00
Price, with 110 volt, 60 cycle Transformer, - - 245.00

tures flickering by on a strip of modern movie film give the illusion of motion.

In the nineteenth century, European inventors came up with various devices that exploited persistence of vision. Most of these devices were considered to be nothing more than toys. One was the *thaumatrope,* which was simply a disk that had on one side, for example, a drawing of a bird, and on the other side a cage. When the disk was spun on a string, the bird appeared to be inside the cage. The *zoetrope* was much more sophisticated; it was a rotating drum with a strip of paper inside showing a series of pictures of some action (like a horse running) in small increments of movement. When the viewer looked through slits in the side of the spinning drum, the horse appeared to move. The strip of drawings was the ancestor of the filmstrip, and the slits were a primitive shutter.

These and similar devices became popular around the middle of the nineteenth century. For the further development of motion pictures, however, it was necessary for the ideas behind these inventions to be combined with another relatively new invention—photography. From the first blurred photographs of the early 1800s, which required long exposure and soon faded, the technology of photography developed until in mid-century, sharp permanent images from life could be captured on paper in exposures of a fraction of a second.

In 1872 the governor of California, Leland Stanford, made a $25,000 bet with a friend. The results of that bet paved the way for the invention of motion pictures. Stanford, a horse breeder and racing fan, bet his friend that at certain points in a gallop, all four of a horse's feet leave the ground. The friend was as certain that they did not, and it was impossible to settle the bet by observing a running horse with the naked eye. Feeling that pictures might prove his theory, Stanford hired an inventor-photographer named Eadweard Muybridge to capture a horse in full gallop.

It took Muybridge five years of experimenting to discover a way to do it. Finally, in 1877, he had a clumsy but workable method. As the horse ran, it tripped strings that triggered, one after another, the shutters of twelve cameras that were lined up along the track. When the resulting stop-action photographs were developed, one showed all four hooves in the air, and Governor Stanford pocketed his $25,000 (he had, however, given four times that much to Muybridge for the experiments). Muybridge had successfully demonstrated that there is a gap between what the mind thinks it sees and what the eye actually perceives.

Over the next two decades Muybridge went on to more elaborate techniques using more cameras, faster film, and subjects ranging from dancing couples to running and jumping athletes. He also invented the *zoopraxiscope*, which could project his photos that simulated movement onto a wall in the manner of a "magic lantern," which had long been used to project drawings.

Now true motion pictures seemed possible, and inventors began to work in that direction. Various inventors solved problem after problem, until the only remaining difficulty was finding a way to link thousands of still images together into a continuous strip. In the 1880s, American inventor George Eastman invented a celluloid film with several individual exposures joined on a single roll for use in his new Kodak still cameras. These largely replaced laborious single-plate photography. Then another great American inventor, Thomas Alva Edison, took the final step.

When he first heard of Eastman's celluloid film, Edison had already developed a camera and tried a number of unsuccessful experiments with moving pictures. Edison immediately realized that Eastman's film could make his experiments succeed and quickly ordered a supply. On January 7, 1894, Edison's chief assistant, William Dickson, filmed the comical sneeze of a laboratory worker. *Fred Ott's Sneeze* thus began the history of true motion pictures.

Over the next few years, Edison and his assistants refined the new invention and created others. Discouraged by the fuzzy images of his first projection machines, Edison for some time favored his single-viewer contraption called the *Kinetoscope*. This was a cabinet containing a fifty-foot loop of film.

While peeping through a viewing slot, the viewer turned a crank to run the film. Each loop, running at 48 frames per second, showed only a half minute of action. By the mid-1890s, "Kinetoscope parlors" had been installed around the country. There, people could insert a coin and view through a peephole films ranging in subject from juggling acts to snippets of dance and romantic scenes.

By the time Kinetoscopes had caught on, however, two French brothers named Auguste and Louis Lumière had invented the first practical projector. The brothers also set the permanent standard of film width at 35 mm and the silent-era shutter speed at 16 frames per second. (They found this was the minimum speed for smooth motion; later, sound films would require a slightly faster speed.) Though most Lumière films were longer than Edison's Kinetoscope loops, they still captured only a few minutes of such subjects as trains entering a station or workers leaving a factory.

By 1896 Edison had developed a true projector, called the *vitascope*. With it, he produced the first public motion-picture performance in America, at Koster and Bial's Music Hall, New York, on April 23, 1896 (a few months after young Sam Goldfish arrived in the city, but fifteen years before he would take note of the new phenomenon). The audience at the Music Hall showing was delighted, though some patrons ducked under their seats when the waves broke on *The Beach at Dover*.

A year later, Edison's first competitors appeared—the American Mutoscope and Biograph Company (founded by Edison's one-time assistant William Dickson) and the Vitagraph Company. These new studios were based in New York, which became the nation's first film center, although most productions were actually shot in New Jersey in such locations as the Hudson River's Palisades cliffs. The new companies came up with innovations both in technology and in approach—more subjects, more

❋

The audience at the Music Hall showing was delighted, though some patrons ducked under their seats when the waves broke on **The Beach at Dover.**

The Squaw Man *company poses outside their studio, a converted livery stable, in 1913. DeMille, wearing hunting boots and breeches, stands next to the star, Dustin Farnum, who is wearing a cowboy hat, chaps, and a long leather vest.*

flexibility in shooting, and the beginnings of developed plots. All filmmakers, however, remained largely bound by the conventions of the stage—sets were obviously artificial, the camera mostly stayed in one place, and actors came and went as on stage, using exaggerated theatrical gestures. Since electric lights powerful enough for filming had not yet been developed, roofless sets were erected outdoors or on top of buildings, and sunlight was used for illumination. The changeable Eastern weather was a continuing problem for filmmakers.

In 1903 an Edison director, Edwin S. Porter, made a historic leap away from the conventional film approach toward a truly cinematic way of thinking with his Western *The Great Train Robbery*. The most elaborate story put on film in the United States at that time, it used techniques which, though to a modern viewer would seem obvious and inevitable, still had to be painstakingly discovered and developed. Most importantly, *The Great Train Robbery* used dramatic cutting from one location to another and from one point in time to another, thereby creating unprecedented tension in its simple tale of outlaws and the posse who followed and captured them. Crude as it is by modern standards, this film laid the foundation of modern film editing.

The sophistication of films gradually improved over the years and nickelodeons sprung up across the United States. By 1910 there were more than five thousand of these little movie theaters in the country, showing films supplied by a growing number of companies. Nonetheless, the business had distinct limitations. The films remained simple, conventional in plot, and one reel (seven to ten minutes) long. The audiences were largely immigrants and working people from the poor neighborhoods of the big cities. Middle-class people tended to disregard the movies feeling that they were an amusement fit for the lower, and illiterate, classes. Respectable stage performers also avoided the screen, believing it unworthy of their talents.

Cecil B. DeMille (1881– 1959). DeMille, who began his career as a theatrical director, moved to Hollywood to direct the first feature-length film, The Squaw Man *in 1913. His last film,* The Buccaneer *was released in 1959.*

Finally the workers, who had been the major audience, began to tire of the novelty of moving pictures. At that point, films were often shown between live acts at vaudeville houses, where they came to be called "chasers" because they were intended to drive the audience out and thus clear the house. When Sam Goldfish emerged in great excitement from seeing his first movies in 1911, he probably did not know that he was thrilled by a business that was then going nowhere.

That same evening, Goldfish burst in on his brother-in-law and shouted, "Lasky, do you want to make a fortune?" Jesse had no objection to that idea,

but when he learned that Goldfish proposed to make the fortune in motion pictures, he was unmoved: "You and I would make a fine pair in that business," Lasky said, "me, a vaudeville man, and you a glove salesman!" He felt this was another of Sam's useless get-rich schemes.

❋

"If you want adventure, I've got a better idea than that. Let's go into the picture business."

Besides, Lasky continued, there was the problem of patent rights. Under the title of the Motion Picture Patents Company, Edison and the other leading film companies had banded together in 1909 to share patents on technology and distribution in an effort to force nonconforming filmmakers out of the business. A theater owner either had to show entirely Patents Company films, which were one- or two-reels only, or none at all. The Trust, as it was usually known, was not above hiring thugs to rough up theater owners and movie producers who tried to get around their monopoly. Jesse Lasky was not about to get involved in *that* kind of mess.

Stubborn as always, Sam pressed Lasky, insisting that if they made better films they could find better audiences and maybe even break up the Trust. The discussion ended with an impatient Lasky telling Sam to go to blazes. There the matter rested for about a year.

Then came another in the chain of coincidences that propelled Lasky and Goldfish into the movie business. Two strangers showed up in Jesse's office and offered him $10,000 to use his name as a trademark for a movie company they planned to establish. Lasky turned them down, but the enormous profits the men had mentioned made an impression on him.

That same night, Lasky had dinner with his old friend Cecil B. DeMille. DeMille was discouraged with his Broadway directing career, and was gloomily talking about going to Mexico to find some adventure fighting in a revolution. Out of the blue, Lasky heard himself say, "If you want adventure, I've got a better idea than that. Let's go into the picture business." DeMille stared at his friend solemnly for a moment, then replied simply, "Let's." From that casual beginning, the two men stepped into film history and began, along with Sam Goldfish, to turn that history in new directions.

On their way out of the restaurant, Lasky and DeMille ran into two acquaintances, Dustin Farnum, an actor, and Edwin Royale, the author of a hit Western play called *The Squaw Man*. On the spot, Lasky bought the play and contracted Farnum for his company's first film venture. That night, Sam picked up the telephone to hear Jesse say, "You win."

In the next months they pooled all the money they could scrape together, including donations from some relatives, and by 1913 had the handsome sum of $20,000 with which to start production. The average cost of a two-reeler in those days was $1,000, so the budget for *The Squaw Man* was lavish for the time. But Sam had already decided that he wanted the company to make feature-length films with fully developed stories. This was a radical step, for it was believed at the time that films longer than ten minutes would not only fail to hold the attention of an audience but might also cause headaches and eventually even blindness.

These notions were disproved in 1912, when another immigrant, a former fur dealer named Adolph Zukor, imported an hour-long film from France. The film was *Queen Elizabeth*, and it starred the great Sarah Bernhardt and supporting players from the distinguished Comedie Française. The film was filled with nineteenth-century theatrical conventions, and Bernhardt's style became absurdly exaggerated on the screen, but her name helped to make movies seem both respectable and artistic. In addition, *Queen Elizabeth* proved that feature-length films were both practical and marketable. From that success, Zukor founded the Famous Players in Famous Plays Company, which later evolved into Paramount Pictures.

Goldfish and Lasky, wishing to profit from the success Zukor had found with features, turned to an American director who had also experimented with a four-reel feature. The film was *Judith of Bethulia* (1914) and the director was young David Lewelyn Wark Griffith, already regarded as the most brilliant man in the business. He had originated many innovations that other directors were picking up including the systematic use of cutting between characters to build tension, the closeup, back-lighting, and the moving camera. (History remembers D.W. Griffith as the man who, more than any other, was responsible for the vocabulary of filmmaking.)

Hoping to sell Griffith on *The Squaw Man*, Goldfish met the director for lunch. Griffith listened as Sam excitedly outlined the plot. Finally Griffith said with great finality, "A very interesting project. And if you can show me a bank deposit of $250,000, I think we might talk." Sam managed not to choke and ended the interview on a friendly note. Immediately after, he offered the directing job to Lasky's friend Cecil B. DeMille, who at thirty-one was an experienced theatrical director but had never laid eyes on a movie set or even a camera. DeMille agreed to a salary of $100 a week.

The partners were in the movie business at last. They called their new venture the Lasky Feature Play Company. Sam was vice-president and business manager; his wife, Blanche Lasky Goldfish, was treasurer. In late 1913 they grandly announced plans to put out a dozen feature films a year.

Actually, the only production in preparation at that time was *The Squaw Man*. It was up to DeMille to produce a hit that would start off the new company successfully. It was up to the partners to find some way around the monopoly of the Motion Picture Patents Company. This solution was simple. They would shoot the film someplace as far away as possible from the New York offices of the Trust.

Chapter 3

So This Is Hollywood

*T*rying to figure out a way to make *The Squaw Man* without running afoul of the Trust and its enforcers, Lasky remembered a town where he had once played on a vaudeville tour: Flagstaff, Arizona. He and Sam decided that Flagstaff would be the ideal place to make the movie. The town was far removed from the offices of the Trust and would certainly be supplied with all the cowboys, Indians, and Western atmosphere any film might require.

In December 1913, Cecil B. DeMille, star Dustin Farnum, and the rest of the company boarded a train for the long ride to Arizona. When DeMille and his entourage emerged from the train in Flagstaff, however, they were greeted by a blizzard, which only occasionally slackened to reveal a featureless flat-land. The director immediately ordered everybody back on the train. They would ride to the end of the line, which was Los Angeles, and then move on to nearby Hollywood.

At that time, the Los Angeles suburb was being developed by the partition of a huge ranch and orchard started by Horace Henderson Wilcox. It was Mrs. Wilcox who named the ranch Hollywood— after a friend's estate in the East rather than the local flora, which included no holly at all. It was not an accident that DeMille had chosen Hollywood. He knew that several movie companies had gravitated to the town, attracted by its year-round good weather and bright sunlight, as well as its distance from the Trust. The first film crew had arrived in town in 1908. Three years later, D.W. Griffith began to shoot two-reelers there. Still, when the Lasky company showed up in 1913, the bulk of American films still came from New Jersey and New York.

In the last days of 1913 DeMille began shooting *The Squaw Man*. Adolph Zukor's Famous Players Company was working in town at the same time, though the two companies never ran across one another. Zukor was making short films, so the four-reel *The Squaw Man* would enter history as the first feature-length movie made in Hollywood.

Filming took six weeks. The rather outlandish plot concerns an Englishman, played by Dustin Farnum, who is unfairly blamed for embezzlement and journeys to the American West, where he falls in love with an Indian girl who saves his life. Farnum's performance would make him one of the screen's first major cowboy stars. (Dubious about the movie business, Farnum had demanded a flat fee of $5,000 for the job rather than the offered stock in the Lasky Company; that decision cost him millions.)

The sets for *The Squaw Man* were built outside a rented stable, which had been converted into a base for the company; horse stalls became offices, projection rooms, and dressing rooms for the stars. Extras were hired off the street and made into cowboys and Indians. DeMille, wearing what would become his

David Wark Griffith (1875–1948). One of the greatest of the early film directors, Griffith's best known films include The Birth of a Nation *(1915),* Intolerance *(1916),* Hearts of the World *(1918), and* Way Down East *(1920).*

legendary attire over the years—jodhpurs, leather puttees, and broad-rimmed hat—learned his trade as he went. He was helped immensely by assistant director Oscar Apfel, who had had some experience in movies, and by stage designer William Buckland, the first art director to be hired for an American film.

Back in New York, Sam Goldfish and Jesse Lasky were equally busy. Using his talents as a salesman, Sam met with the film distributors region by region around the country, persuading them to ignore the Trust and buy exclusive rights for *The Squaw Man*. (At the same time, Sam was still selling gloves—he was not yet secure enough in his movie venture to give up his old business.) Finally, distribution rights were sold for $60,000, for a film not yet finished, made by a new company and an untried director. It was a stunning demonstration of the Goldfish salesmanship. All the partners needed now was the small matter of a presentable film. That requirement nearly ended their game once and for all.

In February 1914, *The Squaw Man* was scheduled for a splashy premiere in California. Lasky went to the West Coast for the event while Sam waited nervously in New York for news of its reception. Finally word arrived that for some mysterious reason there was a problem and DeMille and Lasky were headed East with the film.

When they arrived in New York, all the partners sat down to watch. The movie jumped and fluttered and rolled across the screen in a jumble of cowboys, Indians, and horses. The same problem had wrecked the premiere in California. "We're ruined!" Lasky groaned. Sam Goldfish contemplated, he later recalled, "the wreck of $47,000." The Lasky Feature Play Company was not only facing bankruptcy before the release of its first production, it also was liable to legal action by enraged investors.

With no other recourse, a tearful Sam appealed for help to an old gentleman named Sig Lubin, who ran a film laboratory in Philadelphia and knew more about film technology than anybody else. Lubin's company also happened to be a member in good standing of the Motion Picture Patents Company— the Trust. Whether out of compassion or because he figured this inexperienced outfit was no threat to the Trust, Lubin agreed to help. He took a look at the film. There was nothing wrong with the stock itself; the problem was the sprocket holes. The holes had matched DeMille's cameras but not the projectors, which were not standardized in 1914. The film could be saved by the simple, though tedious, process of hand-gluing new, correctly spaced sprocket holes onto nearly a mile of celluloid. Lubin's technicians did the job with perfect results, made copies of the film, and the Lasky Feature Play Company was in business again.

On February 15, 1914, *The Squaw Man* opened in New York to enthusiastic audiences. Soon it was playing with equal acclaim across the country. A reviewer in *Motion Picture World* observed, "The touches of great beauty contain a secret of success known only to screen presentation—they cause us to surrender ourselves completely to the story . . . and to love this new art form for its own sake."

Those words were prophetic, because a new art form was indeed being born in those years. Overnight *The Squaw Man* made the Lasky Feature Play Company a leader in the film industry and established Cecil B. DeMille as a major director. And, just as important, it cracked the monopoly of the Trust, allowing for a rapid expansion of the film business. *The Squaw Man* also helped to establish the fact that feature-length films were the future of the industry. Shorts would continue to be made for many years, but in 1914 the focus of the business began to shift toward features. The dramatic and visual appeal of the film itself pointed the way to new standards of quality in American movies. Finally, *The Squaw Man* began the real explosion of Hollywood film production; within the next two years, the Lasky and Zukor companies, Charlie Chaplin, and many others would set up shop in town, making Hollywood the film capital of the world.

With the money that poured in from their maiden effort, the Lasky Company plunged into a frantic schedule of simultaneous production and renovation of its Hollywood facilities. The stable-studio was expanded and new buildings replaced orange groves. In 1914 Lasky released twenty-one more titles; the next year they increased to thirty-six. Most of these films were turned out by the unimaginative but efficient Oscar Apfel, who had co-directed *The Squaw Man* with DeMille. The two directors worked together again in the company's second production, *Brewster's Millions,* based, like the first film, on a hit Broadway play.

Like most other film companies, the Lasky Company still looked to the stage for its story lines. Stage plays were used simply because there was as yet little writing specifically for the screen. However, a number of directors, including Griffith, made movies using a simple outline, without a formal screenplay. That process would take some time to develop; meanwhile, the stage seemed to be the closest medium to film and the best source of material. So movies continued in many ways to resemble plays visually—just as, for many years, automobiles looked like horse-drawn carriages.

By the end of 1914, the Lasky payroll included five directors, five cameramen, and dozens of players. The entire industry was thriving—its visibility, glamor, artistic quality, and salaries were growing by leaps and bounds. Now, prominent stage actors began to reexamine their scorn of movies and to board trains from New York to Hollywood.

During this frenzy of expansion, Jesse Lasky moved his family to Hollywood in 1914. Sam's wife, Blanche, and his mother-in-law moved into the Hollywood Hotel. Sam was usually on the road, travel-

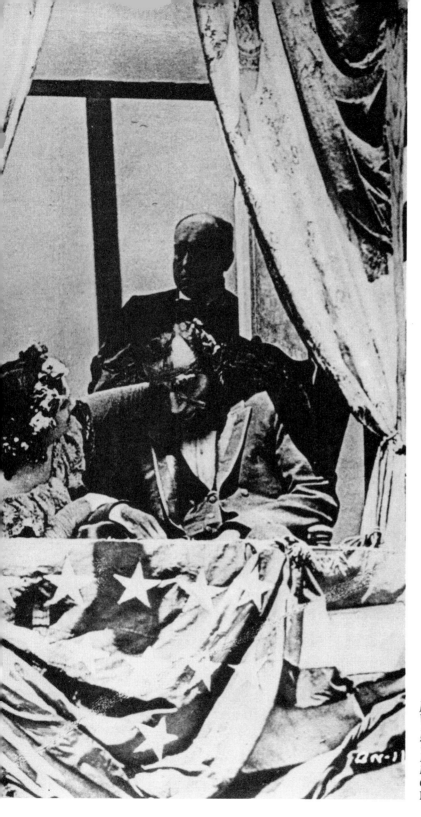

John Wilkes Booth (Raoul Walsh) escapes from the president's box at Ford's Theater, after shooting President Lincoln (Joseph Henabery) in D. W. Griffith's The Birth of a Nation *(1915).*

ing around the country selling his company's movies with the enthusiasm and success with which he had once sold gloves. (He had finally left behind his old trade once and for all.) From now on, the story of Sam's career was also the story of his life, both of them told in a series of movies. He had very little life outside of the film industry.

Though Oscar Apfel turned out the most work for the Lasky Company, it was Cecil B. DeMille who was clearly the most talented director on the lot. Whereas Apfel could produce a feature in three or four weeks, the painstaking DeMille took twice that long. As he gained experience and confidence as a director, DeMille also wrote and edited several of the first years' productions.

With *The Warrens of Virginia* (1915), Cecil came into his own as a director. The screenplay was written by his older brother, William DeMille, a prominent playwright who had not long before tried to talk Cecil out of working in the movies. (William would eventually become a major movie director and producer as well as screenwriter.) Cecil had become dissatisfied with the flat, unnatural lighting all films aimed for in those days. "If an actor was sitting beside a lamp," he later observed, "it was crudely unrealistic to show both sides of his face in equal light." His decision to look for more realistic lighting in *The Warrens of Virginia* was one of many such innovations in the arts that were greeted at first with dismay.

✳

"Aha!" thought Sam: "This is art, this is class!"

To star in the film, DeMille had stolen popular actress Blanche Sweet from D.W. Griffith, paying her an unheard-of salary of $2,000 a week (Griffith had paid $85). To light his pretty star and the other actors, DeMille borrowed spotlights from an opera house and created an unprecedented variety of light-and-shadow effects on the screen. Thus *The Warrens of Virginia* contributed to the art of film lighting.

When Sam Goldfish saw the finished movie in New York, however, history was not on his mind. He was horrified. How, he wired to DeMille, could he expect distributors to buy a film in which you could only see half the actors' faces? Maybe the distributors would only pay half price for the movie!

DeMille and Jesse Lasky put their heads together in Hollywood. Finally they wired back to Sam that people should be able to recognize "Rembrandt lighting" when they saw it—referring to the great painter's use of deep shadows. "Aha!" thought Sam: "This is art, this is class!" "Rembrandt lighting" proclaimed the ads for *The Warrens of Virginia*, and the public was duly impressed.

The year 1915 was a historic turning point in the history of the movies. The turning point was not created by Goldfish and Lasky, but it fit perfectly into their commitment to features. That year saw the premiere of a three-hour epic titled *The Birth of a Nation*, by D.W. Griffith. This story of the Civil War and Reconstruction produced a sensation, compounded partly of justified rage over its pro-Confederate and pro-Ku Klux Klan sympathies, partly of admiration for its brilliance as a battle spectacle and as an intimate human drama.

Goldfish and Lasky, also looking for a new approach to stories to film, began to solicit scripts written not for the stage but solely for the screen. After establishing the industry's first scenario department—headed by William DeMille—they offered a bonus for original screenplays.

One of the first screenplays was Hector Turnbull's script called *The Cheat*. In 1915 Cecil B. DeMille directed this story of a high-society lady who gambles away a fortune and then turns for help to a Burmese playboy. Following the stern morality—and pervasive racism—of movies in those days, she ends up as the vengeful Oriental's branded slave. The film starred stage actress Fanny Ward; the villain was played by the brilliant young Japanese pantomimist Sessue Hayakawa. His restrained, subtle acting style was much admired in a time when most screen per-

Samuel Goldfish with his two operatic stars, Geraldine Farrar (left) and Mary Garden.

formers still used exaggerated gestures. Mainly because of Hayakawa's performance, *The Cheat* proved to be another critical and popular success for the Lasky Feature Play Company.

In the two years since *The Squaw Man* was made, the Lasky Company had become one of the leaders in the industry. Furthermore, the success of films like *The Squaw Man* and *The Birth of a Nation* had transformed the movies from a "cheap show for cheap people" into an art form that had the potential to appeal to every person on earth. The movies were beginning to be seen as reasonably respectable, and highly profitable, work for accomplished stage players. There had been significant technical improvements in the medium as well—in the quality of scenery, art direction, cameras, and film stock, and most of all in the refinement of electric lighting. From its modest origins, the movie industry was becoming a vast and expensive collaborative effort by dozens of artists, technicians, and builders.

Salesman that he was, Sam Goldfish in 1916 pondered the problem of expanding his audience. How could he persuade more of the sophisticated theater-going public to pay to see his company's films? Finally, in one of several experiments carried out over the next years, the Lasky Company partners settled on the unlikely expedient of signing a soprano from the Metropolitan Opera in New York to star in silent films.

This made more sense than it might seem. The diva selected for the experiment was Geraldine Farrar, the greatest American soprano of her day. She was also a vivacious beauty with a romantic aura not often seen in the opera world, and an actress whose talent was remarkable. Among Farrar's stage-door admirers were teenage girls who called themselves "Gerry-flappers."

When the Lasky Company signed Farrar to a three-film, $20,000 contract in 1915, it was expected above all that she would bring glamor and prestige to films. It was hoped that her acting style, though restrained and subtle in comparison with most opera singers, would translate to the screen. There was the problem that the diva, at thirty-three, was older than most movie actresses, many of whom were still in their teens. Also, Farrar was a robust beauty in contrast to the frail and girlish appearance of stars like Mary Pickford and Lillian Gish.

The vehicle chosen for her screen debut was *Carmen*, one of the most popular operas and one readily identified with Farrar. Assigned to write the screenplay, William DeMille discovered, much to his chagrin, that the libretto for Bizet's opera was still under copyright. He had to adapt the original novel by Prosper Mérimée, on which the opera had been based, while trying to keep that fact secret from the public, who thought they were getting the familiar *Carmen*. Naturally, Cecil B. DeMille was assigned to direct the film.

Sam and Jesse were filled with a mixture of excitement and anxiety when Farrar arrived in splendor in Hollywood. Her train was met by the mayor of Los Angeles, costumed cowboys, and five thousand schoolchildren, all of them carrying flowers. On the set, Farrar unnerved DeMille on the first day with innocent observations like, "Why, I didn't realize you had to make a single scene over four times." Soon, however, things were running smoothly— Farrar was not a temperamental prima donna but a hardworking trouper willing to listen to anybody and to try anything. Sam Goldfish adored her, and so did everyone else in the studio.

The results onscreen were more than adequate. After the New York premiere, which was accompanied by an orchestra playing musical selections from the opera, the *New York Times* critic wrote, "This new movie star 'registers,' as the film folk have it . . . Her familiar vigor and dash are helpful, and she can make good use of the flashing Farrar smile." But he felt obliged to add, "Her playing . . . is bold, bald, and in dubious taste." But the public didn't care about dubious taste; Farrar's enthusiastic performance combined with her popularity to fill the houses for *Carmen*.

Farrar went on to work with DeMille in two more Lasky productions, *Temptation* and *Joan the Woman*. Directing her as the French saint in the latter, the director planned a prison scene in which mice would run over Farrar's body. "He was so nice about it," she said, "I couldn't refuse." She was a trouper indeed.

By 1916 the company was well established. All the while, however, Sam's partners—Lasky, DeMille, and old acquaintance Arthur Friend—were finding it more and more difficult to deal with Sam Goldfish. It was Sam's style to be in charge of things, not an ideal personality for anybody's partner. In fact, the others had begun plotting to get rid of him in 1915. The next year, however, a business deal emerged that diverted their attention for a while: the Lasky Feature Play Company was to join forces with its chief competitor, Adolph Zukor's Famous Players. Together, the new partnership expected to become the most powerful film company in Hollywood. Sam, however, simply saw one more partner getting mixed up in his business.

Chapter 4

Goldwyn the Corporation

*I*n July 1916, the Lasky Feature Play Company and Adolph Zukor's Famous Players merged to form the Famous Players-Lasky Corporation. Over the last five years, both companies had grown to be major forces in the movie business and both had pioneered the trend toward feature films. The Lasky Company had the most hits; Famous Players had Mary Pickford, the screen's first superstar, known as "America's Sweetheart." Together, the two companies were a colossus that promised to dominate the industry.

The division of responsibilities in the new company was clearly laid out: Lasky and Cecil B. DeMille were to manage the creative end; the president, Adolf Zukor, and the chairman of the board, Sam Goldfish, would handle business matters. The board of directors was equally divided between representatives of each of the former companies.

In My Best Girl *(1927),
Mary Pickford plays a
shopgirl who falls in love
with the manager's son.*

This tidy arrangement got off to a rocky start,
however. One reason was Sam Goldfish. He was by
nature commanding, demanding, determined to
run the lives of those around him, and quite ready to
throw an extravagant tantrum if he did not get his
way. In short, behind the seasoned business ex-
pertise, calculating intelligence, and sharp show-
business instincts of Sam Goldfish, there remained a
child spoiled by his parents in the Warsaw ghetto.
His wife, Blanche Lasky Goldfish, had put up with
him for only five years before she filed for divorce in
1915. It was a bitter breakup; Blanche began drop-
ping her married name even before the divorce was
final. They had a daughter, Ruth, born in 1911, but
after the divorce, Sam largely ignored her.

Sam was not a particularly vindictive man. He
was capable of generosity and many people over the
years liked, admired, even loved him. His rages
were forgotten as quickly as they began. But he was
not what one would ever call a "nice" person, much

less an easygoing one. He behaved like a spoiled child to the end of his days.

In the first weeks of Famous Players-Lasky Corporation operations, Adolph Zukor got his first taste of the Goldfish style, and did not like what he saw. "Every hour on the hour, and sometimes the half hour," Zukor later wrote, "Sam Goldfish sent a shock through the organization in the manner of those pneumatic drills." Jesse Lasky was long accustomed to handling Sam's temper and his attempts to control every detail; the calm but equally domineering Zukor was not used to it and quickly saw that there was no room in the company for two commanding egos.

It took only a couple of months for the inevitable blowup to occur. It happened after a conference when Sam, in the presence of Mary Pickford, bluntly told Jesse to keep Zukor from interfering in Mary's current picture. Pickford, onscreen the image of Pollyanna sweetness, in real life had a good head for business. She knew Zukor had helped make her the star she was, and now this upstart was trying to keep her old boss at a distance. Pickford went directly to Zukor with the story of Sam's behavior.

Zukor did not lose his temper; he simply wrote Jesse a chilly note: "Famous Players-Lasky is not large enough to hold Mr. Goldfish and myself . . . You'll have to choose between Mr. Goldfish and me." Zukor then left town to await results.

The next few days were very rough for Jesse Lasky. Sam had been his brother-in-law, had dragged him into the movie business in the first place, and together they had risen to the top of the industry. All the same, Jesse was weary of Sam's tantrums, his arguments, and most of all his determination always to be in charge. Adolph Zukor was no saint either, but he was as good a businessman as Sam and far easier to deal with. Lasky finally had to admit to himself, "Sam was not geared to take a back seat to anyone." He found to his surprise that all the former Lasky directors, including DeMille, agreed that Sam had to go.

When Jesse showed up at Sam's suite in the Hollywood Hotel and announced his decision, Sam "turned pale as death." He began to get a little color back, however, when Jesse offered $900,000 for Sam's stock in the company, which would make him a millionaire at the age of thirty-four. The offer was accepted. Jesse probably figured Sam was out of the movie business for good. Famous Players-Lasky Corporation, later renamed Paramount Pictures, would remain a Hollywood kingpin. Jesse's personal success as a producer was to be spotty; despite a few hits like *Sergeant York*, he would end up almost penniless.

The day his old partner fired him was the lowest point in Sam's career, maybe in his life. But there was no holding him down. Within three months, Sam had teamed up with two brothers, named Edgar and Archibald Selwyn, both stage producers, to form a new company called Goldwyn Pictures Corporation. Its name came from the joining of Goldfish and Selwyn. Since there were only two choices for such a combination—Selfish or Goldwyn—the latter naturally prevailed, and Sam got top billing. At first the company was based in Fort Lee, New Jersey, but in 1918 rising costs drove them to California, where they set up shop in a luxurious Culver City studio. As president of the company and chief stockholder, Sam was finally in charge of the entire company.

He insisted on a highly individual approach to talent which would mark the rest of his career—hire the best people money can buy, not only players but also those who work behind the screen. The stable of stars he collected was impressive, though results would be mixed. They included Griffith veteran Mae Marsh, a delicate beauty in the Pickford mold; operatic soprano Mary Garden, who jumped at the chance to follow her arch-rival Geraldine Farrar onto the screen; and Mabel Normand, star of numerous Keystone Cops comedies. Also hired were several prominent playwrights of the time and three leading stage designers. In contrast to the usual casually built movie sets of those days, Goldwyn sets were to be meticulously designed as part of an overall pictorial concept. This concern with production values had considerable influence on the industry; it was also the beginning of what would grow into the "Goldwyn touch."

The new company took a big advertisement in the *Saturday Evening Post* that brashly publicized its collection of talent:

GOLDWYN PICTURES
Brains *write* them. Brains *direct* them.
Brains are *responsible* for their wonderful perfection.

That "wonderful perfection" turned out to be prematurely proclaimed. The first production from the Goldwyn Corporation was a tear jerker called *Polly of the Circus*, starring Mae Marsh. Released in September 1917, the film did well at the box office but was soon forgotten. What success it had was certainly not due to its star. Mae Marsh had given memorable performances in D.W. Griffith's *The Birth of a Nation* and the still grander *Intolerance*, but away from Griffith she was lackluster. Morever, her habit of responding to direction with, "Oh, that isn't at all what Mr. Griffith would do," did not endear her to the Goldwyn Corporation.

If Mae Marsh did not quite pan out in any of her Goldwyn pictures, the contribution of Mary Garden went over the line into disaster. In his memoirs, Sam admitted that when he "reached out toward the far lights of opera and the legitimate drama," he got into serious trouble. His old fascination with the stage and its glamorous players, which had drawn him into show business in the first place, would cloud his judgment for some time.

When he first approached Mary Garden, who was older but more slender than her rival Farrar, she was quite ready to try the screen if Sam's price was right. The soprano's price turned out to be $125,000 for about two months' work. Sam hoped to duplicate the Lasky Company's previous success with Farrar. If Farrar had been introduced with *Carmen,* Garden would make her movie debut with her most famous role, *Thaïs,* for which she had been declared the greatest operatic actress of the age.

Unfortunately, the diva was determined to transfer her opera performance, as the courtesan who is converted to a religious life by love, to the silent screen. That meant extravagant posturings, breast-beating, head-banging, and so on. Word began to go out from the set to Sam's office that Garden was "acting all over the place." It became unintentional comedy.

When Garden saw the "rushes"—daily screenings of new footage—of her death scene, she was appalled at the effect in brutal black and white. "Imagine me, the great *Thaïs,* dying like an acrobat!" she wailed. Bolting from the projection room, Garden ran into actress Margaret Mayo and sobbed, "Did you see the way they made me die? Imagine a saint dying like that!" Responded Mayo drily, "You would have a hard time, Miss Garden, proving to anyone that you were a saint." This did not improve Miss Garden's mood.

The film was completed in an atmosphere of tears, hysterics, and impending catastrophe. Upon its release, the public and critics condemned it, as expected, though everyone agreed that the sets were impressive. Sam Goldfish seized on the one positive point he could find with which to promote *Thaïs*—it was the first motion picture to be screened inside the Vatican in Rome. The film that completed Garden's contract, *The Silent Sinner,* turned out only slightly less awful than *Thaïs,* but the public ignored it. Garden herself called it the worst movie of all time.

The new Goldwyn Corporation made no profit in the Mary Garden debacle, but worse was to come.

Goldwyn produced two even more expensive flops starring much-loved stage actress Maxine Elliott. At the same time, the company stole Pauline Frederick—who was almost as popular as Mary Pickford—from Zukor, only to wrangle with her endlessly about scripts, which she wanted her husband, a screenwriter, to write for the company.

The guiding forces of the Famous Players–Lasky Corporation included (left to right) Jesse Lasky, Adolph Zukor, Samuel Goldfish, and Cecil B. DeMille.

Goldfish again ran into trouble with husbands when he signed up Geraldine Farrar for several more movies. She had married Lou Tellegen, an actor whom she also wanted for her leading man on the screen. Tellegen shamelessly upstaged Farrar on the screen and insisted on top billing in the ads. Farrar meekly agreed. Finally, an embarrassed Sam asked Farrar to let go of the contract before her films and her price wrecked the Goldwyn Corporation. With what Sam described as "the most gallant look in the world," Farrar tore up the $250,000 contract on the spot.

What was keeping the Goldwyn Corporation afloat through all these disasters was a series of low-budget, high-profit comedies starring Mabel Normand. Even that was a mixed blessing, however. Concerned with class and prestige, Sam considered Normand unladylike and her films vulgar. Normand retaliated by calling Sam names and doing hysterical imitations of her boss behind his back.

Class, prestige, public acceptance, a respected name—immigrant Sam Goldfish yearned for those things all his life, giving them more importance than his usual yardstick of success, which was the size of one's salary. Accordingly, in 1918 he got rid of the name he had brought from Poland, which he felt branded him as a poor Jewish kid from the ghetto. It was not that Sam was ashamed of being Jewish, but at a time when American prejudice against Jews ran almost as high as it did against blacks, Sam was aware of the business advantages of downplaying his background. So, completing his personal change of image, he legally took the name of his own company. Henceforth he would be known as Samuel Goldwyn.

Chapter 5

A Turn to the Literary

Now Sam Goldwyn was the boss, in charge of Goldwyn Pictures Corporation, but he was not satisfied. Even though he was president and chief stockholder, he still had partners to contend with—the Selwyn brothers and the other partners and board members who would insist on some power and responsibility. Sam yearned for more independence, and also for the opportunity to create films that were more important than Mabel Normand's comedies and more profitable than the studio's series of prestigious flops.

In June 1919, he announced the formation of Eminent Authors Pictures, Inc., his own subdivision of the Goldwyn Pictures Corporation. The idea was to create a company that "unites in one producing organization the greatest American novelists of today. It ensures the exclusive presentation of their stories on the screen, and each author's cooperation

Will Rogers (1879–1935), folk-humorist and social critic, made twelve films for Samuel Goldwyn.

in production." The writers listed were scarcely the "greatest" novelists of the day, but did include such famous ones as mystery writer Mary Roberts Rinehart and Rex Beach, who wrote highly popular two-fisted adventures.

The first major production of Eminent Authors was *Jubilo* (1919), a Western tale that introduced Will Rogers to the screen with a modest box-office success. The plot was adapted directly from a magazine story after Rogers rejected an Eminent Authors screenplay—a portent of problems to come. After he was discovered by Rex Beach working in a stage review, Rogers did well enough in *Jubilo* to create a career in films, including twelve for Goldwyn, but he would find his true niche as a master of sociopolitical humor until the coming of sound.

In the end, though, few Eminent Authors pictures would have much impact on the box office or on the critics. The only notable one besides *Jubilo* was *The Penalty* (1920), a thriller remembered exclusively for the performance of Lon Chaney as the legless "Blizzard."

The main problem with Sam Goldwyn's bright idea of hiring prominent novelists to raise the level of screenwriting was that a screenplay is a very different proposition from a novel or a stage play. Few people understood this concept in 1919—least of all the Eminent Authors. These novice screenwriters expected the finished products on the silent screen to be faithful renditions of their word-bound stories. For example, one writer included in his scenario the direction, "Words fail to describe the scene that follows." He did not realize that it was his job to describe the scene. Another innocent wrote in his script, "Not by accident, they found themselves alone in a cabin in the mountains." It took the unhappy director, William DeMille, two weeks and five sets to invent and shoot that "not by accident."

Goldwyn's new writers also tried to turn the clock back and make movies more like plays. The creators of the film medium had spent two decades painstakingly developing techniques of shooting and editing that were appropriate to the screen. As William DeMille wrote of the Eminent Authors, "The gentlemen from Broadway decided at once to disregard such picture technique as we had been able to evolve and follow more closely their rules of the theater. They thought the whole idea was to photograph a play very much as it would be performed on the stage. They . . . rejected [the screen's] few hard-won assets."

Those assets included: the ability to move nearer in to see a character's face in closeup, letting the expression show what a writer would have to spell out; cutting instantly from place to place to create dramatic tension and visual rhythm; and using grand effects of outdoor space. The public, finding that Eminent Authors consisted of standing

Lon Chaney (1883–1930), known as the 'Man of a Thousand Faces' often portrayed grotesque characters.

in rooms speaking inaudibly at one another, was not inclined to enthusiasm about the "wonderful perfection" of Goldwyn pictures.

On the studio lot, the writers were strangers in a strange land. The movie people tended to treat these new faces as intruders, and what was done to their stories appalled all the Eminent Authors. Perhaps the oddest case concerned the legendary Belgian poet Maurice Maeterlinck, who had won the Nobel Prize in literature and whose masterpieces included the romance *Pelleas and Melisande* and the immortal fairy tale *The Blue Bird*. Goldwyn made an offer to Maeterlinck during the poet's visit to New York. Attracted by the shining possibilities of the film medium and the siren call of Sam Goldwyn's money, the very eminent writer, who spoke no English at all, journeyed across the continent to Hollywood. Sam somehow arranged for the trip to be made in President Woodrow Wilson's personal railroad car.

With the aid of an interpreter, Goldwyn tried to impress Maeterlinck with the names of the other Eminent Authors. Learning that the poet had never heard of any of them, Goldwyn remarked testily, "What is he, a dumbbell?" (It is hoped the interpreter did not translate.) Things went quickly downhill from there. When his first story, a fantasy concerning a boy with blue feathers, was summarily rejected, Maeterlinck tried to come up with something more realistic. This proved to be a racy story of an extramarital romance, but without the necessary moralistic ending. In desperation, the studio spent days running popular films for Maeterlinck. This immersion in the commercial worked too well: the brainwashed poet produced a script that was pure melodrama. Soon a thoroughly confused Maeterlinck was on the train back to New York. Another of Goldwyn's efforts to gain prestige had failed.

Writer Mary Roberts Rinehart was far more experienced in the ways of the world than the dreamy Maeterlinck, but Hollywood still managed to shake her. Arriving on the lot the first day, she was immediately taken into the makeup department, and then perched on horses, fences, and directors' chairs for publicity photos.

When the thoroughly disoriented Rinehart finally was allowed onto the set to watch the filming of "her" story, she could not find the remotest resemblance to what she had written. "When I threatened to become violent," she recalled, "I received a box of flowers!" Needless to say, her Hollywood career was an extremely short one.

Rinehart's screenplay had gone through the typical Hollywood script mill, in which many people handled a story, each contributing his or her own ideas, good or bad. Goldwyn was quite aware of this problem; in his memoirs he described the process: "Is it any wonder that of the original story bought by the editorial department, perhaps one idea survives the general assault? For by the time that you have wheedled your actress into accepting 'Mary Had a Little Lamb,' the director decides that a goat possesses infinitely greater revenues of humor. Then the editorial department, conceding the goat, insists on an alteration in the type of heroine. She becomes 'Hildegarde, the girl with a punch.' After this everybody thinks up so much business for the goat while he is on the road that, of course, he never gets to school at all. He probably lands at Coney Island, or, better still, in the lobby of a fashionable hotel. Of one thing you may be certain: the terminus will be some place where Hildegarde can wear all her latest Paris gowns and wraps."

For a good many reasons, Eminent Authors Pictures, Inc., was not a success. However, as with many of Goldwyn's ideas, both profitable and unprofitable, in the long run Eminent Authors made significant contributions both to motion-picture art and to Sam Goldwyn's development. It raised the status of the screenwriter and convinced many in the industry that good movies must begin with strong stories and screenplays. An overriding concern with a tight story line and clear dramatic development would mark Goldwyn productions from then on.

Such emphasis on the story was to have good and bad effects on the future of Goldwyn's films. On the one hand, it gave Goldwyn productions a characteristic thrust and drama that helped make them both effective and popular, and that fact had its influence on the entire American film industry. On the other hand, it tended to make character development and insight subordinate to the plot. Ultimately, it would be European films (or European directors working in America) that would bring psychological insight to the screen.

Though one of the screenwriters, Rupert Hughes, went on to write the Goldwyn hit *The Old Nest* and later became a director, most of the Eminent Authors soon left Hollywood in disgust. The response of Rex Beach was typical: "We were to be paid a certain stipulated sum during the term of our contracts, whether our work was acceptable or not. As far as I am concerned, that agreement was faithfully kept. And that is the only thing I have to say about the life of a helpless author on the Hollywood lot."

The screenwriters who grew up with the industry in the early decades of the twentieth century were not great poets or writers, and rarely first-rate playwrights. Instead, they were people of talent who learned how to write specifically for the movies. From the beginning it was a business in which women were accepted and excelled. By the mid-1920s, screenwriting would be an established craft and profession.

America's involvement in World War I in 1917 and 1918 created a war-oriented market in which many movie companies went out of business. Sam kept Goldwyn Pictures afloat through that period with a series of brilliant, if nerve-wracking, financial deals. The threat of disaster seemed to bring out the best in him. While Sam was rescuing the company, however, he continued to fight with his partners. The Selwyns and the other backers, unnerved by Sam's abrasiveness and his financial dealings, voted him out of the Goldwyn Corporation. Sam managed to persuade them to take him back.

After the war, Goldwyn unleashed a flood of productions—twenty-three in 1920—designed for wide audience appeal and quick profits. This effort was largely successful, helped by an ad campaign that sold the studio's product to ordinary Americans: "When you see a Goldwyn picture you forget your troubles—you forget the baby's croup and the cook's leaving."

While this spate of minor but profitable productions got the company back in fair financial shape, it did not improve the position of Sam Goldwyn in the company. In 1922 Francis Joseph Godsol became a vice-president and executive committee member through connections—including a relative—on the committee. Godsol was a flashy international playboy and something of a con man. His main ambition was to get rid of Samuel Goldwyn and take over the company.

Encouraged by Godsol, the board of directors began to lean on Sam to be more forthcoming about the complex of deals, expenditures, and future plans for the company. Sam was not inclined to respond to these amateurs pushing into his business. But the board had ammunition to use against him: Goldwyn Pictures Corporation was showing a profit but Eminent Authors—Sam's brain child—was floundering. Also, in 1920 Sam had made a major miscalculation in arrangements for European distribution that had cost the company heavily. At that point, the board came up with a reorganization plan that threatened Sam's power. In response he at first resigned, then immediately rejoined the company.

As these developments were shaking the stability of the Goldwyn studio and the nerves of its executives, Sam came up with yet another of his brilliant and farsighted ideas, in which once again he contributed to the history of film while losing money. This time, he would lose his job as well.

Some German films had been successful in America in the previous decade, so Sam had been watching for new imports that also looked promising. One German production that caught his eye was *The Cabinet of Dr. Caligari* (1919). The story concerns a mad doctor who keeps, inside a cabinet, a zombielike creature who goes out and murders people on the doctor's orders. There was nothing remarkable in the story, but the scenery, designed to be a reflection of the mad doctor's mind, included painted sets that were a dizzying maze of distorted buildings and jagged streets in impossible perspectives. The movie consisted of real people moving about in a surrealistic world.

It is not likely that Sam Goldwyn appreciated the deeper implications of this film; psychology and

The Cabinet of Dr. Caligari (1919) was a successful German horror film that was very innovative in its surrealistic set design. Goldwyn bought the rights but the film did not do well here.

experimental art were not his strong points, and he was far from being an intellectual. However, as a producer who recognized the importance of art direction, he knew a new and interesting approach to set design when he saw it. So he bought the rights to *The Cabinet of Dr. Caligari* and mounted a big New York premiere in April 1921.

Most critics were enthusiastic about the film. *The New York Times* review stated, "The picture is significant . . . because . . . all of its elements, its settings, its plot, its people, are expressive [and] eloquent." Other critics called the movie a major advance in the art of film. (History would remember *Caligari* as a brilliant and influential dead end—there was no future in surrealistic scenery, but a great deal—as Sam Goldwyn understood—in expressive set design.)

Most of the moviegoing public did not care a great deal about art, history, or innovation. Rather, they wanted to be moved, excited, titillated, amused, or scared in the most direct way possible. So the public did not care for *The Cabinet of Dr. Caligari*. The premiere was enlivened by boos from the audience and dozens of viewers noisily trooping out of the theater to demand their money back. Possibly it was the critics alone who sat through the whole thing. Results were the same wherever the film was shown.

It was perhaps Sam's most conspicuous debacle yet. Theaters showing *Caligari* lost audiences for that and later films. Some sued the Goldwyn Corporation, and Joe Godsol had his opportunity to get rid of Sam Goldwyn. In March 1922, Godsol engineered a vote of company stockholders that forced Sam out, giving him an even million dollars for his stock. (Within two years of Sam's departure, the floundering Goldwyn Pictures Corporation would be bought out in turn by the Metro company, and both would then merge with Louis B. Mayer's studio to form Metro-Goldwyn-Mayer. Many people would thereafter wrongly assume that Samuel Goldwyn was a co-founder of MGM.)

It had been quite a career for a film czar so far. In ten years, Sam had helped build two major studios and had been fired from both of them. It would seem that he was a spectacular failure as a businessman, though each failure had left him a million dollars richer.

Amazingly, the first thing Goldwyn did after being pushed out was to procure a large advance from a publisher, hire a ghostwriter, and produce his memoirs. The result, published in 1923 as *Behind the Screen*, might have told a fascinating story of a journey from the Warsaw ghetto through a troubled marriage and business career, to riches and fame. Instead, on the whole the book was disappointing; among many other omissions, it makes no mention whatever of Poland, his Jewish background, his wife or his child, or even the name Goldfish.

Rather than a searching autobiography, the book was actually a publicity campaign designed to lay the foundation for his next foray into the movie business. The next time, though, he would find his place in the industry once and for all—and there would be no one to fire him because he would own the whole company, lock, stock, and barrel.

Chapter *6*

Samuel
Goldwyn
Presents

*T*he advent of a new motion-picture company was announced in 1922: Samuel Goldwyn Productions, Inc. Its namesake was owner, sole stockholder, board of directors, banker, talent scout, creative consultant, and anything else he chose to be. Now the movies with his name on them were really going to be "his," paid for out of his own pocket. Technically speaking, Sam was now an *independent producer*—which meant he was the boss, the employer, the person who raised the money and attempted to see that it was wisely spent. That is why over the next three decades he would have the freedom to, as he put it, "make my pictures to please myself."

The frequent clashes between producers and directors symbolize the eternal divide between business and art in the movie industry. The producer can never forget that a film is an extravagantly expensive

The stars of Stella Dallas
*(1925) were Belle
Bennett, Ronald Colman
(center, who played her
husband), and Jean
Hersholt (who played the
other man in her life).*

venture and that one major flop can ruin a studio.
Meanwhile, the director, obsessed mainly with the
quality and impact of his or her work, is constantly
demanding more time, more sets, more extras, and
more independence.

Though producers are the directors' lifeblood,
the thing filmmakers fear above all else is that the
producer will try to get involved in the actual filmmaking; the blackest days in the business are those
when the producer shows up on the set. Directors
often create elaborate ploys to keep bosses at bay.
When Orson Welles was making his great *Citizen
Kane*, the cast and crew were ordered to stop work
and start playing baseball whenever a producer
appeared. At around the time he started directing
for Sam Goldwyn, King Vidor complained in an arti-

cle, "The final decisions [in Hollywood] are made by business men, not artists . . . [the producer], with his lack of visual imagination, is not able to fill in the gap between the scenario and the finished article. Consequently the order that each detail of the script be so obvious and overwritten that . . . the ultimate whole is all too obvious and dull."

As in most things, Sam Goldwyn was an exception to these rules. His films were profitable enough to make him, in the end, one of the two most successful independent producers in the history of Hollywood (the other was David O. Selznick, who made *Gone with the Wind*). Besides his generally solid business and commercial instincts, Sam would involve himself very much in the creative side as well. Most of his movies' story ideas originated with him. If a story did not appeal to him (and, later, to his second wife), it was not made. This was also true of his choice of stars and directors.

Of course, the people he hired actually made the movies, and like all creative people they did their best to resist the interference of their boss. Goldwyn was unusual in showing some respect for that creative independence and in giving his filmmakers a comparatively free hand.

William Wyler (1902– 1981) directed many of Goldwyn's greatest films, including Wuthering Heights *(1939),* The Little Foxes *(1941), and* The Best Years of Our Lives *(1946).*

The basis of his approach was very simple, and had characterized his approach to producing from the beginning: hire the very best people you can find, pay them well, and encourage them to do their best. The people who would work for Goldwyn over the years included director William Wyler, cameraman Gregg Toland, screenwriters Lillian Hellman and Ben Hecht, and actors like Ronald Colman, David Niven, Lucille Ball, and Danny Kaye.

Goldwyn held his creative people on relatively loose reins and yet his pictures had a unique style that came to be called the "Goldwyn touch." Studios like MGM and Warner Bros. would concentrate on glamor and slickness. Goldwyn concentrated on achieving an exceptional level of quality and maturity. The "Goldwyn touch" involved fine craftsmanship in cinematography, editing, and lighting, and a strong story line—often dealing with unusually serious or controversial themes, but put into a package that was still entertaining. Though later standards of frankness would make his controversial films seem rather tame, the most memorable Goldwyn pictures were stories with a hard edge and a good deal of social consciousness: *Stella Dallas* (1925), *Arrowsmith* (1931), *Dodsworth* (1936), *Dead End* (1937), *The Little Foxes* (1941), and above all, *The Best Years of Our Lives* (1946).

It's hard to say how Sam managed to use the strong personalities of his creative people and inspire them to develop the "Goldwyn touch," as he worked in the screening room, on the lot alternately coddling and bullying his directors and stars, supervising story conferences, and overseeing the various other divisions of filmmaking.

In 1922, with the creation of his own production company, Sam was in the market for a studio. He turned to United Artists, which had been founded by D.W. Griffith and Charlie Chaplin, Mary Pickford, and Douglas Fairbanks, Sr., three of the leading film actors. This group of superstars who had founded their own company appealed to Sam's independent tastes, and they were happy to rent him space in their studio. Following further negotiations, United Artists agreed to release and distribute Goldwyn films, three or four a year, for some time to come.

At the same time that Sam was setting up the new company, his former partners were taking him to court. Goldwyn Pictures Corporation did not want to see "Samuel Goldwyn Presents" on his new studio's films, even if that was now his legal name. After much negotiation, it was agreed that Sam could indeed put "Samuel Goldwyn Presents" on his ads and title cards—as long as he added below those words, in letters of equal size, the qualification "Not

Now Connected With Goldwyn Pictures." When the floundering Goldwyn Company was absorbed into MGM, that studio sued Sam for the same reason. The result of that case was an agreement that he would always include his first name. Now, at any rate, "Samuel Goldwyn Presents" could stand alone in screen credits—which at times would involve the formula "Samuel Goldwyn Presents . . . A Samuel Goldwyn Film . . . Produced by Samuel Goldwyn." (Understatement was never a Goldwyn trait.)

His first release with the new company was *The Eternal City* (1923), a melodramatic tale of Rome, directed by George Fitzmaurice, who specialized in exotic adventures, and starring Lionel Barrymore, Barbara La Marr, and Montagu Love. The movie, which presented a favorable view of Mussolini's Italian fascists, did not receive good reviews and only a fragment of it has survived. Its value today is as a novelty, revealing a popular opinion in the United States in the 1920s.

The same year, Goldwyn scored a hit with *Potash and Perlmutter*, the first of three comedies featuring the clashes of two partners in the clothing business. Successful as they were at the time, the films did not add luster to Goldwyn's reputation. His next project, however, would be the most memorable film he had yet produced—*Stella Dallas*.

The story, taken from a best-selling novel, was familiar to nearly everybody at that time. Stella is a good-hearted poor girl who marries a rich husband, but is never able to change her simple ways. She ends up rejected by both husband and daughter. In the pathetic conclusion, a forgotten and destitute Stella secretly watches the wedding of her daughter to a wealthy young man. It was the sort of story known in the trade as a "four-hankie weeper."

Stella Dallas had the potential for melodramatic overplaying, but Sam found the right director for the project—Henry King, the first of the great directors who would work for Samuel Goldwyn Productions,

Inc. over the years. King was especially admired for the warm human touches in his films—the dramatic effect of a look or a sigh. He also had a keen cinematic sense, learned from D.W. Griffith. This visual brilliance would make King a master of his craft, and an inspiration to Russian film theorists, who were intensive students of American techniques. In 1921, shortly before Goldwyn signed him up, King made one of the great silent classics, *Tol'able David*, a story of American small-town life. Goldwyn knew that film, but what had mainly caught his eye was another picture directed by King, *The White Sister* (1923), starring Lillian Gish and a young British actor named Ronald Colman. Goldwyn hired both King and Colman and put them to work for him.

Henry King treated *Stella Dallas* with subtlety and restraint and made the picture into both a minor classic and a major box-office success. The wedding scene at the end was particularly moving. When he saw it, Sam dissolved in tears and cried to the director, "I can't stand it! You've ruined me! An audience can't stand all this emotion!" A couple of days later, Goldwyn had recovered sufficiently to insist that King add a scene in which an alcoholic character suffers a spectacular case of delirium tremens. This was done, using special effects which cost an additional $30,000. When the results were seen in place in the film, though, hardly anybody liked the scene. Neither did Sam, and it was cut.

Goldwyn's new leading man, Ronald Colman, had worked on the British stage and made several minor films in England before emigrating to the United States. When Henry King spotted Colman in a play and approached him about movies, Colman was dubious; someone had told him that two small scars on his face made him unsuitable for the screen. King had the actor grow a moustache, rearranged his hair, starred him in *The White Sister*, and one of the movies' most beloved figures was created. For many years to come, Colman would handle a wide variety

Fay Wray and Ronald Colman costarred in The Unholy Garden *(1931).*

of roles with unflappable suavity and class. He was considered one of the screen's great gentlemen, whether playing detective Bulldog Drummond, Sidney Carton in *A Tale of Two Cities*, or Conway in *Lost Horizon*.

Goldwyn claimed to have discovered all of his stars; in fact, most of them were discovered by his directors. But on a trip to Europe, Sam did find Vilma Banky, a graceful young Hungarian actress whom he brought to the United States for a few years of glittering success before the coming of sound to films ended her career. Goldwyn starred Colman and Banky, whom Goldwyn publicists dubbed "The Hungarian Rhapsody," together in their first American film, *The Dark Angel* (1925). That and later costarring roles with Banky established Colman's career, made the two one of the classic romantic duos of the silent screen, and made millions for Goldwyn. A whole generation of young men and women wanted to be like Colman and Banky.

Always on the lookout for material to give his "love pair," Goldwyn seized on a popular Western novel called *The Winning of Barbara Worth*, paying author Harold Bell Wright the unheard-of sum of

$125,000 for the screen rights. To write the scenario he picked Frances Marion, one of the new crop of outstanding women screenwriters. Henry King was to direct. Besides putting the best talent he had into the picture, Goldwyn was banking on a climactic special-effects sequence—a spectacular bursting dam and subsequent flood.

The magic didn't quite happen, however, although the film *The Winning of Barbara Worth* turned out to be one of the greatest box-office hits of 1926. History, a more exacting audience, remembers the picture mainly for the screen debut of Gary Cooper, which came about by a remarkable chain of coincidences.

The romantic leads for *Barbara Worth* were Colman as a mining engineer and Vilma Banky playing a double role as a woman who dies on the desert and her daughter Barbara Worth. Goldwyn had hired a youthful actor to play the important supporting role of Abe Lee. That actor was finishing up a film at Warner Bros. but promised to be done in time to take on the part.

As Henry King was getting ready to start filming in Hollywood, he noticed Gary Cooper sitting gloomily outside the casting director's office clutching a film can. Cooper had already failed to impress anybody at the studio with a cheap screen test he had had made of himself. His previous screen experience was as an extra in low-budget Westerns. Seeing King, Cooper leaped up to make one more try: he wanted to play the part of Abe Lee, the second lead, in *Barbara Worth,* he said; would King please take a look at his test? King shook his head and said he'd already signed someone for the part, but promised to have a look at the screen test.

A few minutes later, King was looking at an amateurish piece of film with an amateurish actor riding up on a horse, jumping off with a stunt spill, looking seriously into the camera, and then breaking into a wide and undeniably pleasant grin. King was not particularly impressed, but didn't see why Cooper couldn't handle one of the bit parts in the movie. He decided to hire him for fifty dollars a week.

Shooting began. For one scene, King told Cooper, who was standing in the background of the shot, to keep his eyes on Vilma Banky. Cooper proceeded to stand on one spot for the entire day without once taking his eyes off the leading lady, whether the cameras were rolling or not. Well, concluded King, this kid might be inexperienced and he might be dumb, but he's ready to do anything.

Meanwhile, the actor hired to play Abe Lee was still busy at Warner's. So King let Cooper stand in as Abe for a few scenes. By the time the company headed West for location shooting, the director was beginning to be impressed with this young man. He decided, as an experiment, to try Cooper in the part's big scene, in which after being injured in the flood, Abe Lee rides across the desert to die in Ronald Colman's arms.

On the desert set, King accosted Cooper one morning, smeared his face with wet clay, and began to walk him up and down, around and around, talking to Cooper about being tired, about being exhausted, about being bushed, done in, played out. All morning Cooper walked while King departed to shoot a scene and then returned to apply more clay and talk about how Abe Lee was absolutely weary unto death.

As for the scene itself, the director told Cooper (who had never read the novel) to knock on the door, with great weariness, and, when Colman opened it, to stammer a few words and then fall like a log, flat on his face. "Yes, sir," gasped Cooper, "I'll do it."

Now that Cooper was suitably exhausted, King set up the shot. Suddenly there was a summons from Sam Goldwyn, the kind of summons that a director knows is big trouble. The director walked to meet Goldwyn like a schoolboy heading for the principal's office.

※
The director walked to meet Goldwyn like a schoolboy heading for the principal's office.

Gary Cooper in The Winning of Barbara Worth *(1926) with Vilma Banky.*

"Henry," roared Sam, "when you spend a dollar of my money, you're spending a dollar of your own!" When King inquired as to the meaning of this mysterious proverb, Goldwyn replied, "You're putting that damn cowboy into one of the biggest parts in the picture! How are you going to do the big scene? No damn cowboy can play it!" King explained to his sputtering boss that the actor they'd hired to play Abe Lee had still not arrived, so they were "just using up some film" in trying the scene with Cooper. Goldwyn retreated, saying, "You're just teasing, Henry. You just do everything to *tease* me!" King hurried back to the set.

To his relief, King found that his cowboy was still exhausted. By now Cooper had so much clay crusted on him that he already looked like a ghost. He knew what he was required to do for the scene, but had no idea how Colman and another actor were to respond. On the shout of "Action!" he stumbled to the door and knocked. Recalled King years later, "I don't think anything will remain in my memory as long as the sight of Gary Cooper standing full length in that door, looking across the room and saying, 'Mr. W-W-Worth . . .'—and falling flat on his face. As he went down, Ronnie Colman and Paul McAllister grabbed him, and Cooper's face missed the floor by two inches."

King hastened to set up Cooper's death scene, a closeup in bed. At that point came another summons from Sam Goldwyn. Knowing he had to get the scene done while the actors were still hot, the director rushed off with great anxiety. This time, Goldwyn raved, "Henry, why didn't you tell me that man was a great actor?" Sam had been peeping through a hole in the curtain as Cooper did the scene. Now Sam was ready to offer this newcomer a contract. Fine, King said, but "unless we shoot this scene, we won't have a picture." He rushed back to finish the scene, then told a jubilant Cooper that he had won the part of Abe Lee.

A star was about to be born, but Sam Goldwyn would be a little too slow on the draw to realize it. When *The Winning of Barbara Worth* was completed, clearly destined to be a hit whatever its flaws, Henry King told Goldwyn assistant Abe Lehr that he ought to hire Cooper at $100 a week. Lehr replied that this might spoil the kid, and offered $75. While Cooper was thinking that over, someone at Paramount saw his performance in the movie and offered him a contract at $750 a week. Cooper's meteoric rise at Paramount would be the cause of much pain to Sam Goldwyn, and he would spend years angling to get the "damn cowboy" back.

Sam may have let a major new talent slip through his fingers, but he had once again started

Samuel Goldwyn Presents

Sam and Frances Goldwyn with Sam Jr. in 1926.

off a new company with a good run of hits: his third try in the movie business was going to be the lucky one. He would find equal success with his second try in marriage.

Frances Howard McLaughlin had arrived in show business pursuing the trades of showgirl and model. This led to a couple of performances on Broadway as a "flapper"—one of the hell-raising, gum-chewing, bobbed-hair adventurous young women of the Jazz Age. Her stage roles, which were far from her personal style, brought Frances to the attention of Jesse Lasky, who signed her to a Paramount contract and first starred her in an adaptation of Ferenc Molnar's *The Swan* (1925). Many years later, this same story of a prince torn between royal marriage and a commoner would mark the final screen appearance of Grace Kelly before she married Prince Rainier of Monaco.

Sam had first met Frances when she was presented to him as a possible starlet. He had curtly dismissed her because "I don't like bobbed hair." At their second meeting, at a New York cocktail party, she apparently looked a great deal better. Certainly he was taken by her beauty; perhaps the fact that he might steal her from his old partner Lasky made her still more attractive.

They were married three weeks after they met. Frances immediately gave up her acting career and moved with Sam to Hollywood. A son, Samuel Goldwyn, Jr., was born the following year. Their marriage was to be happy and fruitful in more directions than their child. Sam was one of the world's most self-centered and difficult men, and hadn't the slightest understanding of women; but Frances would do far more than keep his house and put up with him—she would become his main business partner.

The Movies
Are Reborn

When Frances McLaughlin married Sam Goldwyn in 1925, she was joining forces with one of the most successful men in one of the richest businesses in the country. The movies had come a long way in the eleven years since *The Squaw Man*. By 1925 silent films had become big business, screen stars were considered to be virtual gods and goddesses and commanded fabulous salaries, and the majority of Americans of all classes—and a great percentage of the rest of the world—went to the movies regularly. Long before television appeared and radio was widespread, motion pictures were the first universal artistic medium, available to everyone, without the barriers of language, distance, or money. As such, they had an immense influence on American society, not only in fashion, but in the evolution of ideas and moral standards. The movies not only popularized the flapper's bobbed hair, short

Looking east on Hollywood Boulevard, 1934.

dresses, and the Charleston, but also her fast-and-easy lifestyle and attitudes.

From the outset, sex appeal was one of films' main stocks-in-trade. In the early years men yearned for delicate beauties like Lillian Gish and Mary Pickford, a contrast to the "vamp" (short for vampire) Theda Bara. In the 1920s, they were superseded by the pouting Clara Bow. Meanwhile, women developed passions for such heroes as William S. Hart and John Gilbert and especially for Latin lovers like Rudolph Valentino and Ramon Novarro.

Movies, as much as any other factor, changed American culture from the attitudes and styles of the Victorian era into the modern age. The screen brought all kinds of people together and thereby helped to break down social barriers. It provided fresh, new ideas about work and the role of women in society, and it gave everyone an image of the good life. The movies reflected society, its beliefs, and trends, but the film industry also had begun to change society. That was something Sam Goldwyn understood as well as anybody.

Sam and Frances lived the glittering life of a movie mogul. They had a big house in Hollywood, near the studio, and another in Santa Monica, on the short stretch of beach where Chaplin, Pickford, Lasky, and other film people had houses. Every member of this film colony competed with the others to throw the biggest, most expensive, and extravagant parties, and to secure the most glamorous guest list, preferably including a European princess or two.

Hollywood acquired its reputation as the capital of the rich and carefree. The one-home suburban ranch had become the legendary land of Hollywood, though those residents who stopped working and partying long enough to think about the place were not always starry-eyed about it: "Nothing here is permanent," lamented David O. Selznick. "Once photographed, life here is ended." And Ethel Barrymore was even tougher: "The people are unreal. The flowers are unreal; they don't smell. The fruit is unreal; it doesn't taste of anything. The whole place is a glaring, gaudy, nightmarish set, built up in the desert."

The gaudy life was not the Goldwyns', however. Their parties were a little tamer, and gatecrashers were resisted. The most typical Goldwyn evening was an elegant dinner party, to which only selected guests were invited; some people, like Walter Brennan, worked for Sam many years without an invitation. Sam had long been a devotee of fine clothes, one of the dressiest men in a very dressy town. He never carried cash because a wallet would disturb the smooth lines of his trousers and jacket.

Every workday, Sam walked several miles to and from work, striding vigorously down the street while his limousine crept after him at a discreet distance. This walking, plus workouts at a gym, kept him in unusually good health for most of his life and gave him the energy he needed to maintain his grip in the film business. Photographs of him all show the same trim, broad-shouldered, elegantly dressed figure.

Sam never lost his early love of the theater. To the end of his days he spoke enthusiastically of Sarah Bernhardt and the other stars of his youth. In the 1940s, screenwriter Garson Kanin remembered going to a ballet performance with Goldwyn. As they entered the theater, Sam reminisced about hearing Caruso and Mary Garden and Geraldine Farrar sing opera in that same theater, and after the ballet Kanin was surprised to see his boss weeping over Margot Fonteyn's dancing in *Giselle*.

Goldwyn was never known to read a book; the ones he bought for his pictures had to be narrated to him by employees or by his wife. He worked on his English constantly, eagerly picking up and practicing new words, and over the years he became reasonably articulate.

All the same, his English remained heavily accented and entirely his own. And there remained his legendary blunders of grammar and logic. At a meeting to discuss labor and union difficulties, for example, Sam is reported to have said, "Include me out!" The usual term for such remarks is *malapropism;* around Hollywood, however, they were affectionately dubbed *"Goldwynisms."* The list of these is endless, some of the most famous including: "I can answer you in two words—im possible." "I'll give you a definite maybe." "Directors are always biting the hand that lays the golden egg." Of a script: "I read part of it all the way through." On *The Best Years of Our Lives:* "I don't care if it doesn't make a nickel. I just want every man, woman, and child in America to see it." On the progress of time: "We have all passed a lot of water since then." And most celebrated of all: "Anybody who goes to a psychiatrist should have his head examined."

Nobody knows which Goldwynisms were actually uttered by Sam Goldwyn. After a few of them were heard in Hollywood, people began to make up their own (Lillian Hellman, for example, invented the one about the psychiatrist.) Moreover, for some time, Goldwyn's press agent was actually assigned to make up Goldwynisms and feed them to the newspapers as a publicity stunt. Goldwyn also had a disconcerting inability to remember the names of his employees. Danny Kaye reported that in his first three years at the studio, Goldwyn persisted in calling him "Eddie," presumably confusing Kaye with Eddie Cantor. Sam assured a novelist dubious of his future in films with, "If you write two or three successful pictures, the name of Bloomfield will be known all over the world." The writer was Louis Bromfield.

In later years, when Sam's English had improved and he was more concerned with his reputation as someone who associated with world leaders, he tried to refute the Goldwynisms. It didn't work, not only because the phrases had become part of Hollywood lore, but also because Sam was still given to talking faster than he was thinking: "Don't talk to me about Goldwynisms, f'Chrissake," he grumbled to one writer; "You want to hear Goldwynisms, go talk to Jesse Lasky!" Another Goldwynism.

Lillian Hellman once said, "To understand Sam, you must realize that he regards himself as a nation." A nation does not have to bother about minor matters like grammar or a person's name. Sam Goldwyn felt that what he was doing—making pictures—was the most important thing in the world, and everybody around him was expected to feel the same way. That meant that they had to put up with whatever he wanted. Often as not, they *did* put up with it, partly because they were being paid extravagantly, partly because they knew he was often right, partly be-

※
"Anybody who goes to a psychiatrist should have his head examined."

cause Sam was seen as a bit more honest, less of a con man, than most Hollywood producers.

In 1927 the silent screen, and Sam Goldwyn, were at the peak of their power and wealth and popularity and artistry. At that point, however, the industry was about to be shaken to its core, and then to be reborn—the movies were about to start talking.

Of course, silent movies were never really silent. There had always been a pianist or an organist or an orchestra in the theater, musically underlining every action and emotion in the picture. Speech and sound had been heard in experimental productions almost from the beginning. In 1895 Edison's assistant William Dickson had shown his boss a film of himself raising his hat and speaking. But the process had proven unsatisfactory and Edison decided to leave films silent. The optical sound track system that was eventually to be adopted for film was invented in the first years of the century. For some time, however, those working on the problem of sound preferred the phonograph, another relatively new invention, a method that had problems synchronizing two machines to make sound fit with image.

In the 1920s the Warner Bros. studio seized on the novelty of sound in hopes of improving their shaky fortunes. The studio released *Don Juan* (1926) with sound effects in what they called the "Vitaphone" process. In this process, large records that played for one reel, were synchronized with the picture—theoretically synchronized, that is. One sound engineer recalled a character in a Vitaphone short opening his mouth and emitting the sound of a banjo. Meanwhile, the Fox Company was experimenting with a sound-on-film process called "Movietone." This optical sound track alongside the pictures was far easier to synchronize and within a few years would become the standard method.

Warner Bros. began the sound revolution. In 1927 the company decided to risk its financial neck on the world's first feature with spoken dialogue—

The Jazz Singer, which starred blackface vaudevillian Al Jolson. At the New York premiere on October 6, 1927, Jolson spoke from the screen, "You ain't heard nothin' yet!" He also sang and spoke a small amount of dialogue. Though the film was not totally dubbed, his line was prophetic.

The public flocked to see *The Jazz Singer,* but critics and the industry were cautious at best, deeply upset at worst. The movie magazine *Photoplay* called *The Jazz Singer* "Al Jolson with Vitaphone noises," and predicted, "The 'talking picture' will . . . never supersede the motion picture without sound. It will lack the subtlety and suggestion of vision."

Like most producers, Goldwyn at first hoped that this new fad would simply go away. Screen players, who had perfected and made their fortune on the difficult art of silent-screen acting, were terrified. Goldwyn received a letter from Ronald Colman saying, "I would rather not sign this [contract], at any rate, just at present. Except as a scientific achievement, I am not sympathetic to this 'sound business.' I feel . . . that it is a retrogressive and temporary digression insofar as it affects the art of motion-picture acting—in short, that it does not properly belong in my particular work."

Since Colman was an experienced stage actor with a beautiful voice, his letter is an astonishing document. In later years, Goldwyn was fond of showing the letter around, to demonstrate how resistant even the best-prepared artists were to the coming of sound.

Producers are in the business of gauging which way the wind is blowing, and in 1928 they began to notice that the worst of the new talkies were doing better business than the best of the new silents. Goldwyn held out though that year, worried especially that Vilma Banky's thick Hungarian accent would ruin her in sound films (which is just what happened). During this year he made two more silents starring Colman and Banky and in *This Is*

The Jazz Singer (1927), starring Al Jolson and May McAvoy, revolutionized the film industry. Few people remember that although this was the first 'talkie,' a great part of the film was silent.

Heaven (1928) experimented with sound effects and dialogue. Finally, in 1929, when industry profits on sound pictures had nearly doubled the take of silents in 1927, Goldwyn joined the sound revolution.

Goldwyn's first all-talkie was *Bulldog Drummond* (1929) which starred Ronald Colman as a dashing detective. Despite his reservations about sound, Colman immediately revealed himself as a great speaking actor on film. He was perhaps the first screen player to stop projecting, which was necessary on the stage, and to address the microphone intimately. The result was that his rich, cultivated voice fit perfectly with his gentlemanly image. The role brought him his first Academy Award nomination.

Bulldog Drummond also marked the debut of Joan Bennett, who would later become one of the leading ladies of the screen. The script was by an eminent playwright, Sidney Howard, and to do it justice Goldwyn broke with the silent practice of staging a film with the cameras running. The entire production was rehearsed ahead of time, like a play, and that procedure was followed in most future Goldwyn pictures.

Before microphones became portable and cameras quiet, early talkies tended to be static and rather dull. While the noisy camera rolled in a soundproof booth, characters often sat at a table chattering earnestly into a bouquet of flowers, in which the microphone was hidden. So critics were quick to praise *Bulldog Drummond*'s quick cross-cutting and mobile camerawork for bringing some movement and action back to the screen. Though it is still somewhat primitive by today's standards, this is one of the first talkies to appeal to modern audiences.

Over the next few years, Hollywood exerted its considerable ingenuity in improving sound. Somebody put a microphone on the end of a broom handle and thereby invented the boom mike, enabling actors to walk and talk. Quiet cameras emerged from the soundproof booth so that they could move again—in panning and tracking shots or mounted on cars. By the mid-1930s, movies had regained the movement and flexibility that the silent screen had achieved, and the sound revolution was complete.

The year of *Bulldog Drummond*'s release was also the year of the great stock-market crash and the beginning of a bitter, decade-long economic depression. Fortunes vanished overnight as banks collapsed, formerly comfortable families found themselves standing in soup lines, millions were destitute and homeless. Paradoxically, though, during the 1930s, movies became more successful. The screen became the primary means of escape from grim reality. Hungry Americans were happy to pay one of their last quarters to see Fred Astaire and Ginger Rogers dance across elegant rooms, to see Clark Gable or Cary Grant in action.

Sam Goldwyn's contribution to escapist entertainment was two musicals (a form with which he would have little success). His first musical, *Whoopee* (1930), was done with the aid of master showman Florenz Ziegfeld, whose *Ziegfeld Follies,* featuring lots of pretty girls dancing in skimpy costumes, were a longstanding Broadway tradition. Flo had his Ziegfeld Girls; Sam therefore decreed a bevy of Goldwyn Girls. In the end, *Whoopee* fell short of reproducing the Ziegfeld magic onscreen, though the star, Eddie Cantor, and the choreographer, Busby Berkeley, who were making their film debuts, had great futures in musicals. Cantor would work for Goldwyn in a series of very popular comedies; Berkeley, his wilder ideas vetoed by Sam through four productions, would depart for Warner Bros., where his kaleidoscopic routines, with their overhead shots of twirling dancers, would grace some of the most memorable musicals of the 1930s. Busby Berkeley's last Goldwyn film was *Roman Scandals* (1933). Goldwyn started with a perfectly good script by two masters, George S. Kaufman and Robert E. Sherwood, and then added more jokes by other writers. However, the Goldwyn Girls, wearing less than ever, made script problems irrevelant, and Cantor was at his comedic best.

It seemed that with the advent of talkies, Goldwyn was floundering, perhaps losing his famous "touch," even if he was still making money. In fact, he was on the verge of his golden years, when he would produce some of the most striking and successful films in the history of Hollywood.

Chapter 8

A Social Conscience

*I*n 1930 Sam Goldwyn had a stable of players headed by Ronald Colman, now one of the leading actors of the day, and Sam was determined to get all the mileage he could out of his elegant star. Colman appeared in *The Devil to Pay* (1930) and *Raffles* (1930); in the latter he played a dandy who also happens to be a thief. Next year came a far more memorable production—*Arrowsmith*, based on a Sinclair Lewis novel about an idealistic physician. This picture, one of the first enduring classics to come from the Goldwyn studio, demonstrates both the strengths and the failings of the "Goldwyn touch."

As usual, Sam started with a strong, carefully considered script, written by Sidney Howard. The plot concerns a young doctor, Arrowsmith (Colman), who marries a small-town girl Leora (played by Helen Hayes) and gives up his dream of doing medical research to practice in his wife's hometown. Before long, disgusted by a narrow-minded veterinarian who rejects his successful cow vaccine, Dr. Arrowsmith and his wife leave for New York and he rejoins his old teacher in a research company. When Arrowsmith develops a vaccine that apparently can cure a plague raging in the West Indies, he and Leora go to the islands and he begins an experiment. He innoculates only half the natives, saving their lives. The other half act as control and are not vaccinated. Only that way can the doctor prove scientifically that his vaccine works. When his wife dies of the plague, however, Arrowsmith decides to innoculate everyone, choosing to save lives instead of advancing his scientific career.

The burning moral issues *Arrowsmith* addresses may not seem shocking or unusual these days, but at the time they were sensational. Moreover, the picture had farsighted racial attitudes. One of the secondary characters is a black doctor who is portrayed with great sympathy and dignity. In the film generally, the lives of the suffering black natives genuinely matter—they matter as much as any lives do, and matter enough to turn Dr. Arrowsmith from a scientist into a genuine humanitarian.

If *Arrowsmith* were simply a matter of progressive social conscience, it would not be as effective as it is to audiences today. The real reasons for its success, in its own time and later, are the stong performances of Colman, Hayes, and several supporting players, and the striking visual appeal that director John Ford brought to his first Goldwyn film.

Today, Ford is best remembered for his Westerns, beginning with the classic *Stagecoach* (1939). But Ford did more than set the pattern of the Western: he brought a strong visual and dramatic sense to all his films (even though, astonishingly, he was half blind and had to wear dark glasses).

Part of *Arrowsmith*'s effect is a result of the rich atmosphere John Ford created, especially the piercing sunlight and textured shadows of the tropics. The film received an Oscar nomination in 1932 and became a perennial favorite.

Arrowsmith was the first of several Goldwyn productions that examined current social and ethical questions. In later years, though, when such concerns became commonplace, some critics accused Goldwyn's serious films of lacking commitment. In Sinclair Lewis' original novel, for example, the doctor leaves his wife's hometown in disgust at the petty qualities of the whole place. Goldwyn and screenwriter Howard dropped that aspect since Sam reasoned that it was a distraction in the plot. Also he did not want to offend paying moviegoers in small towns.

True, the treatment of black people in the film was courageous in a time when Southern theaters were known to boycott pictures that showed a favorable view of blacks. The portrayal of a black doctor in the film was a risk. But the blacks in the film were West Indian, not American, so they did not aggravate the South's racist feelings. Lewis' book was bitterly critical of the whole medical profession; little of the criticism ended up in the film.

In its time, *Arrowsmith* was an unusually serious and advanced film in its social views, to the point of being controversial; however, Sam Goldwyn stopped at exactly the point where the film might have been *too* controversial. Later critics accused him of hiring the best artists and then watering down their ideas to make them more commercial.

Goldwyn had two contradictory intentions in the movie business: the desire to stay in business by making profitable films, and in the process to make himself as wealthy and prominent as possible. The way to do that was to give the public what it wanted. As Sam once told an interviewer, "If the audience doesn't like the picture, they have a good reason. The public is never wrong . . . The public pays the money. It wants to be entertained. That's all I know."

Ronald Colman played an idealistic doctor in Arrowsmith *(1931). Helen Hayes played his wife.*

And another time he dismissed social messages in movies with, "Messages are for Western Union."

If that was all Sam Goldwyn really knew, however, he would not have gained the respect he did from the public, and from many critics, and from history. Instead, he would have made more and better clones of *Whoopee* and *Roman Scandals*. Many producers have made more money than did Sam Goldwyn by doing just that.

Goldwyn wanted more than riches and fame. He wanted respect, and most of all he wanted to make genuinely good pictures. So he went for both at once—successful entertainment *and* quality. In his best films, starting with *Arrowsmith*, Goldwyn and his creators would indeed achieve both. As Goldwyn's admirers point out, perhaps an entertaining film with wide appeal can best put across a serious theme to the general public. Only about half of Gold-wyn's films actually made a profit, which is a fairly good record in Hollywood. Studios survive mainly because a very few films make spectacular profits.

The next major production was *Street Scene* (1931), which marked the Goldwyn debut of director King Vidor. Sam had tried without success to hire Vidor a decade before, when the director was barely out of his teens and was already recognized as a major talent. Since then, Vidor had made some silent classics, including *The Big Parade* (1925) and *The Crowd* (1927).

Street Scene was based on a successful stage play about adultery and murder in a New York tenement. The author, Elmer Rice, had been one of Goldwyn's Eminent Authors. Like most of the Eminents, in those days Rice had been dismayed to find that the finished films barely resembled the stories he had written. When Goldwyn made his generous offer for the play, Rice asked, "If you have some other story in mind, why don't you hire someone to write it, instead of wasting your money on *Street Scene?*" When Goldwyn protested that he *did* want to make *Street Scene*, Rice replied, "That's all I'm asking you to do." Thereupon Sam hired Rice to write the screen adaptation, which was just what Rice had wanted.

Following Goldwyn's standard procedure, Vidor rehearsed the cast before bringing them onto the set, a city streeet built in a sound studio. The finished movie was impressive in the way the camera explored the limited environs of the set, photograph-ing it from striking angles. The public enjoyed it, and *Street Scene* joined *Arrowsmith* as one of the major hits of the era. The maturity of subject in both those films brought new respect to Sam Goldwyn. Government film censorship was about to clamp down on the screen, however, so thereafter until the 1960s, most sex, immoral behavior, and violence in films would have to be read between the lines of the script, or in the look of a character's eye.

King Vidor (1894–1982). Vidor's best films included the silent classics The Big Parade *(1925) and* The Crowd *(1927).*

As soon as King Vidor finished *Street Scene,* he began *Cynara* (1932), again starring Ronald Colman. Like *Street Scene,* it was based on a play concerning extramarital affairs. Colman's character, a British lawyer, has a romance with a young shopgirl, but returns to his wife. At that time, there was a peculiar double standard governing adultery in the movies: the woman who strayed with a married man had to be killed off. The man could be forgiven, but the adultress had to die. So, in *Cynara,* the shopgirl kills herself as a result of the good-hearted lawyer's misguided attempts to be a gentleman about the affair.

A critic astutely summed up *Cynara* this way: "A Frenchman would have made [the story] into high comedy but this serious and sympathetic handling gives it powerful appeal for the women fans and therein lies its prospect for commercial success. That and the genuinely moving sincerity of its acting."

The series of eighteen successful films Colman made for Goldwyn came to a sudden halt with *The Masquerader* (1933). This was a lurid story from a turn-of-the-century novel which had been filmed several times before. Colman played two roles, a journalist and a drug-addicted politician. Goldwyn's publicity department released a statement, supposedly by Sam himself, saying that Colman was especially good at playing dissipated parts, and in fact acted better when he had been drinking. Colman, a true professional and not particularly fond of drinking, was outraged. Not caring if it was simply a publicity stunt, Colman sued Goldwyn for libel and asked for two million dollars in damages.

It is not clear if Goldwyn deliberately insulted Colman for some obscure reason by implying that his star acted best when drinking. Sam could have apologized. Instead, he fought the suit before settling out of court by paying Colman an undisclosed sum. Not surprisingly, the actor refused to work out the remaining two years of his contract. Sam retaliated with the traditional threat, "You'll never work in this town again!" Eventually released by Sam from his contract, Colman played his greatest roles for other studios—Sidney Carton in *A Tale of Two Cities* (1935) for MGM and Conway in *Lost Horizon* (1939) for Columbia.

Even without Colman, Goldwyn was very successful. He felt it was time to build a still bigger house for his family, and left the project to Frances, knowing she would understand what he wanted. He was not disappointed in the result. The gigantic white Hollywood mansion had a kitchen able to handle the largest dinner party, a gym, a projection room, and an office. In keeping with his new position in the world, Sam began to speak more slowly and carefully in public, and sometimes would refer to himself as "Mr. Goldwyn." And he would live up to his new pretensions. The next years would see his greatest screen triumphs.

Chapter 9

Romance and Realism

By 1935 Sam Goldwyn employed a staff of artists, designers, and technicians that rivaled any in the business. He relied on this assemblage of talent for the simple and astonishing reason that he knew very little about the technical side of his own business. Money and its manipulation he understood very well indeed, but he probably had only a hazy idea of the workings of a movie camera.

For that reason, Sam could provide little supervision on his productions until he saw something onscreen. At that point he would say what he thought, shooting from the hip, often in very roundabout fashion. He might not be able to identify what was wrong with a scene or a sequence or a picture, but his judgment was often sound and, of course, as the owner of the studio he was the final authority. It was up to his employees to understand what he wanted and to try to execute it—all in all, a very unscientific way to run a business. Sam's artistic instincts helped his company to prosper, but they also could land him in trouble—especially in the matter of leading ladies.

A vital part of the "Goldwyn touch" was cinematography, the art of the cameraman, a field that was constantly evolving as new technology developed. Goldwyn's director of photography, Ray June, won an Oscar for his work in *Arrowsmith*. The man who would be most associated with the studio in the 1930s and 1940s, however, was Gregg Toland.

Toland was obsessed with his craft, continually experimenting with lenses and film and lighting effects. He could give a character a spiritual or supernatural glow, could make a room look candle-lit. Above all, he perfected the technique of deep-focus photography, in which the camera could keep both nearby and distant objects in sharp focus at the same time. Toland's deep-focus photography in Orson Welles' *Citizen Kane,* made when he was on loan to RKO, is his most famous work, although he began to experiment with the technique in earlier Goldwyn films with William Wyler. Over the years, deep-focus would change the art of film, making for a richer visual texture. This in turn led to longer and more complex single shots, replacing the older method of continually chopping up the action into small shots. Gregg Toland worked for Goldwyn for twenty years.

Another long-time Goldwyn employee was Danny Mandell, one of the most respected film editors. A studio director rarely had the final say on how a movie was put together, and the way thousands of separate strips of film were joined could affect the meaning and quality of a picture. Mandell often worked with Goldwyn looking over his shoulder. Watching a sequence onscreen or sitting at the little Moviola editing machine, Sam would make suggestions about pacing or whom to highlight.

Sometimes Mandell would object, and a brisk shouting match would ensue. (Sam's best people were the ones likeliest to stand up to him; he seemed to appreciate the strength of their opinions.) By the end of Danny Mandell's career, he had won three Oscars for editing—for *The Pride of the Yankees* (1942), *The Best Years of Our Lives* (1946), and the non-Goldwyn production *The Apartment* (1960), for United Artists.

Another element in the "Goldwyn touch" was costume designer Omar Kiam, whose personal costume design included capes and a gold-headed cane. He excelled at exotic pictures like *The Adventures of Marco Polo* (1938). Kiam's employment at the studio ended abruptly, though, during the production of *Wuthering Heights* (1939), when at a Goldwyn party he drunkenly spilled a goldfish bowl over Sam and Frances.

Art director Richard Day designed the sets for many Goldwyn productions, including the memorable city street in *Dead End*. Day won Academy Awards for Goldwyn's *The Dark Angel* and *Dodsworth*, and for five other films. Set decorator Julia Heron was a master of researching period details and collecting the dozens of small items that give a set authenticity. Determined to be accurate in every detail, she fought with William Wyler when the director wanted furniture of decayed oak for *Wuthering Heights* (1939). Heron insisted "that furniture *never* goes to pieces" and refused to see it looking fragile.

Any film is a cooperative effort of writers, directors, performers, designers, editors, and dozens of other craftspeople and artists. Goldwyn, by virtue of his bank account and despite his demanding presence, was able to employ people who were at the top of their professions.

Most of Goldwyn's films of the late 1930s and 1940s would fall into two categories—contemporary realism and literary romance. There would be successes and failures in both categories.

Now and then in the course of his career, Goldwyn seemed to warm up for big successes with spectacular failures. In 1933 he created a major problem when he discovered in a German film an actress he was convinced would rival Greta Garbo and Marlene Dietrich.

The actress' name was Anna Sten. She had been born in Russia and trained there for the stage under the legendary Konstantin Stanislavski. After making some silent films in Russia, in 1930, the soulful actress emigrated to Germany where she made several sound pictures, including a version of the classic Russian novel *The Brothers Karamazov*. It was her performance in that film that so impressed Sam, who believed she would be his greatest discovery, the actress of the century. He signed Sten to a contract in 1932 and brought her to Hollywood.

The next two years were spent trying to coach Sten to speak English intelligibly and carefully choosing and shaping the story for her American debut. Finally, Goldwyn chose *Nana*, an adaptation of the classic French novel by Emile Zola. In the original book, Nana is a high-class prostitute who dies miserably of smallpox. This was not the sort of story in which Goldwyn wanted to introduce his glamor girl; besides, censorship required by the new Hays office created by the movie studios themselves to censor objectionable behavior and language from the screen would never pass such a story. (Screen censors would exercise an iron rule for about thirty years, ensuring that American movies stayed in a dream world where all crooks were caught, nobody used bad language, endings were almost always happy, and babies apparently were brought by the stork.)

Under the circumstances, one might well ask why Sam picked *Nana* for Sten in the first place. In any case, by the time he and his screenwriters got through twenty-five drafts of script, the heroine had become a glamorous and quite unreal lady of myste-

rious employment who dies a suicide—without
dirtying her glorious costumes. It was the kind of
movie in which well-dressed aristocrats are always
raising champagne glasses to the heroine. It had so
little resemblance to the original novel that the title
credits confessed the story was only "suggested" by
Zola.

Despite the best efforts of director Dorothy
Arzner (then the only woman director in Hollywood), plus Gregg Toland's photography, the stun-
ning sets, and a $40,000 barrage of publicity, few
people were ready to swallow this version of Zola.
The publicity brought in record crowds for opening
night at New York's Radio City Music Hall; but when
reports went out from critics and viewers, business
declined. The realistic acting style and earthy beauty
of Anna Sten would have been perfect for Zola's
original *Nana*, but it was all wrong for this sanitized
and prettified version. Besides, there was the matter
of her heavy accent, which had resisted two years of
vocal coaching; at times onscreen, she seemed not
even to know what she was talking about. As songwriter Cole Porter wrote, "If Sam Goldwyn can with
great conviction/Instruct Anna Sten in diction/Then
Anna shows/Anything goes!"

Sam's obsession with Sten and *Nana* had caused
an epidemic of frayed nerves, ulcers, and nervous
breakdowns around the studio, but despite the failure of the film, Goldwyn was by no means ready to
give up. He put Sten into a second picture as extravagant as the first. This time, she starred in a Russian
story, Tolstoy's *Resurrection*, although the title was
changed to *We Live Again* (1934). He asked Dorothy
Arzner to direct, but she wisely declined. The directing job finally went to Rouben Mamoulian. Also
Russian-born, he had recently directed Greta Garbo
in *Queen Christina* (1934).

Once again, the mighty resources of the Goldwyn studio and publicity department supported the
production. Costarring with Sten was distinguished

actor Fredric March, who proved to be quite unhappy with the whole affair. "Cheer up, Freddie," said Sam to the gloomy March on the set, "You got the best part in the picture." Then he turned to Miss Sten and added diplomatically, "And you, Anna, you got the best part too!"

The ads for *We Live Again* assured the public, "The directorial skill of Mamoulian, the radiance of Anna Sten, and the genius of Goldwyn have united to make the world's greatest entertainment." When he saw the ad, Sam was enthusiastic: "That's the kind of ad I like. Facts, not exaggeration." The public did not quite agree. A few were willing to grant that this new Sten picture was an improvement over the last one. All the same, it was another star-studded flop. Anna Sten was beginning to be known as "Goldwyn's Folly."

Persisting in his folly, Sam decided to make one last effort. Having gone nowhere with a French and a Russian novel, he hired writer Edwin Knopf to write an American story specifically tailored to Anna Sten, which became *The Wedding Night* (1935). The director was King Vidor and for leading man Sam borrowed the services of Gary Cooper, whom he had let go to Paramount a decade before.

The very unlikely story of *The Wedding Night* had Sten as a betrothed Polish-American farm girl in Connecticut, who falls in love with a married city writer played by Cooper, who returns her affection. The screenplay solves the dilemma of their impossible romance by the too-convenient device of having the farm girl accidentally fall down a flight of stairs to her death.

The picture was made in an atmosphere of extreme tension. Director Vidor felt that getting Sten to speak intelligible English was impossible. Sam showed up on the set to give pep talks, suggesting that if the picture was not a hit they were all ruined. Of one love scene, he roared to the befuddled cast, "I tell you, if this scene isn't the greatest love scene ever

put on film, the whole goddam picture will go right up out of the sewer!" Critics said that it was the actress' best job yet, and some admired Vidor's direction and especially Gary Cooper's performance. By now, however, few moviegoers were willing to see an Anna Sten picture. It was another two million dollar loss, and that was about as expensive as a picture got in the 1930s. Hollywood would call *The Wedding Night* "Goldwyn's Last Sten."

In later life, Sam would privately admit, "I must've been *crazy* that year . . . I don't know much about baseball, but I know that three strikes is 'out.' So we had a few meetings . . . Anna and her husband and me. And we all decided we should call it quits." (Sten would make six movies for other studios, all of them flops.) Philosophically, Sam continued, "I want to tell you something about this business. Nobody *knows* anything. You can think and you can feel and you can believe, but you can't *know* . . . I have to guess. I have to please myself, that's the main thing."

Goldwyn's Russian discovery, Anna Sten, made her American film debut in Nana *(1933).*

Sam's instincts would never again fail him as badly as they did with Anna Sten (though his choice of actresses would never be as good as his choice of actors or directors.) In 1936, the year after *The Wedding Night* debacle, William Wyler started working for the Goldwyn studio.

Wyler had been born in Germany, studied violin in Paris, got interested in movies, and came to the United States in the early 1920s to work for Universal. Working his way up from desk jobs to directing, he served his apprenticeship in the last years of the silent era. When he first went to work for Sam Goldwyn, he had a modest reputation. With the aid of cinematographer Gregg Toland and the other resources of the Goldwyn studio, he became a first-rate director.

His first film for Sam, *These Three* (1936), set the standard. Actually, it set several standards—for striking direction by Wyler, for solid writing by young playwright Lillian Hellman, and for resourceful avoidance of the censors.

The problem was that the original plot of *These Three*, to be adapted by Hellman from her own play *The Children's Hour*, involved a child who falsely accused two of her women teachers of being lesbian lovers. When Hollywood heard that Hellman had convinced Sam to buy the play for $50,000, the town was convulsed with laughter. Goldwyn could not use the story or even mention the title onscreen, because the play was so notorious. Whether true or not, word went around that when told the story was about lesbians, Sam innocently replied, "That's no problem; we'll change them to Americans."

In her screenplay, Hellman deftly toned down the controversy simply by switching the sex of one of the accused and making the situation into a triangle; now the child was falsely accusing two teachers, a woman and a man engaged to another woman, of having a heterosexual affair. In those heavily-censored days this all had to be understood between the lines. The stars included leading man Joel McCrea, while Goldwyn favorite Merle Oberon played the wronged fiancée and Miriam Hopkins the accused lady.

Despite a tacked-on happy ending, the film turned out rather well. Though it would seem, like so many controversial films of the 1930s, tame to audiences accustomed to far more frankness, the film made its impact at the time: novelist/critic Graham Greene wrote of *These Three*, "I have seldom been so moved by any fictional film . . . One [saw] . . . a genuine situation, a moral realism."

As many viewers noticed, the film also shows a brilliant joining of Gregg Toland's camera work and William Wyler's gift for human touches, the small gestures and moments that add up to a fine emotional realism. Wyler achieved this quality the hard way, by riding his cast like a martinet, demanding so many retakes that he became known as "90-take Wyler." Another director of the era, W.S. Van Dyke, earned the nickname "One-Take Woody" on films like *The Thin Man* (1934).

Somewhere in all those retakes, Wyler would find a striking quality, perhaps an accidental event that revealed something meaningful about the character. In *The Best Years of Our Lives* (1946), for example, an inexperienced (and handicapped) actor stumbled over his lines in a wedding scene; Wyler used that take, knowing the mistake would underline the character's nervousness. On the set, performers tended to loathe the director. David Niven, who made one of his first screen appearances in *Dodsworth*, recalled that leading lady Ruth Chatterton once slapped Wyler's face and fled. With Niven, Wyler usually sat beside the camera reading a newspaper through take after take, looking up only to bark "Do it again!" Niven said the experience turned him into "a gibbering wreck." When they saw the results and began to reap the accolades, however, performers were ready to work for Wyler again.

Dodsworth (1936) was a Wyler picture made the same year as *These Three*, and it too turned out to be one of the most celebrated films to come from the Goldwyn studio. Based like *Arrowsmith* on a Sinclair Lewis novel, *Dodsworth* had already been made into a Broadway play.

Its subject was the disintegration of a marriage, once again for Goldwyn, an unusually realistic and controversial subject for the time. On a European trip, Midwesterners Sam and Fran Dodsworth began to have marital troubles, mainly due to Fran's infatuation with sophisticated European men. As a result of her foolishness, she drives her husband into the arms of another woman. As Walter Huston observes in the film, "Love has got to stop someplace short of suicide." The critics were very impressed, *The New York Times* expressing its "complete satisfaction" with every aspect of the picture. A large part of its effect came from leads Walter Huston (father of director John Huston), Ruth Chatterton, and Mary Astor in one of her most engaging other-woman roles. Though the film won only a single Oscar for Richard Day's art direction, *Dodsworth* was nominated in seven categories, including best picture, director, actor, and screenplay.

The immediate public response to *Dodsworth* was muted; stories of marriages falling apart were not box-office favorites. Instead, the film had a long-term success, building its audience over time. Forty years later, a Hollywood film-festival audience would give it a standing ovation. Not used to long-term successes, Sam would alternately describe *Dodsworth* as one of his best pictures or as a disaster.

In any case, Goldwyn could neither congratulate nor blame himself for the fate of the picture. Early in 1936, as he was preparing for the production of Wyler's first Goldwyn films, Sam was stricken with terrible pain on a ship from Europe. He was carried ashore near death with what proved to be a severe gall bladder attack.

Chapter *10*

Goldwyn's Heyday

*I*ronically, Sam Goldwyn's best years in the movies began as he lay in the hospital in great pain from his inflamed gall bladder. Slowly, he began to recover and return to business.

During the first period of recovery, he opened his eyes one day to find an ominous figure dressed in black standing beside his bed. He finally realized that it was Sarah Lasky, mother of both his former partner Jesse and his ex-wife Blanche, who died of pneumonia in 1932. His furious ex-mother-in-law had some demands. If he lived, Sam was to recognize his and Blanche's daughter Ruth, whom he had always ignored; and furthermore, he was to take Ruth's husband, McClure Capps, and their child into the family and care for all of them. Weak and sick as he was, Sam could not resist. He also agreed that Ruth's husband, an artist, could work for the studio. Capps was hired as an assistant art director and turned out to be a very capable one. From the day of that visit, Sam's condition began to improve. After several weeks in a New York hospital, he returned home to Hollywood. At the end of the summer he had another crisis that required gall bladder surgery and an appendectomy, but his recovery continued.

Through the months of his convalescence, the studio was run by Merritt Hulburd, who acted as producer while William Wyler was making *Dodsworth*. Sam, as soon as he was over the crisis, began (despite doctor's warnings) to demand daily reports and to badger his employees from his bedside. Before long, Merritt Hulburd was feeling the heat, with Sam questioning every detail. Finally, Hulburd fled the studio. Sam was frantic, calling around until he reached Hulburd and shouted into the phone, "Merritt, how can you *do* this to me? You are my *wife*, Merritt!" (Hulburd quit a year later. The following year he died at age thirty-five).

The filming of *Dodsworth* continued smoothly in Sam's absence. An equally promising script called *Come and Get It* (1936), however, did not fare so well. It was assigned to director Howard Hawks, who had made the successful melodrama, *Barbary Coast*, for Goldwyn in 1935. Things were going well enough until Sam learned that Hawks had made unauthorized changes in the script. Sam summoned the director to his bedside and angrily demanded that the script be filmed as written. Hawks refused and quit the picture.

Still bedridden, Sam pressured an unwilling Wyler to finish *Come and Get It*. This time Sam became so enraged that Wyler bolted from the house. Finally forced by his three-year contract to give in, Wyler reshot much of *Come and Get It* at a cost of half a million dollars. Not surprisingly, the result was disappointing. Nonetheless, it was very successful at the box office, and Walter Brennan won an Oscar for his supporting role. And Sam, despite all his rages—or maybe because of them—continued to get well.

In 1937, fully recovered, Sam was back in his office at the studio, and things began running normally (never smoothly with Goldwyn in charge). There were some strong productions in preparation, the first being a film adaptation of a remarkable play called *Dead End* (1937). A long-running Broadway hit despite its grim realism, *Dead End* was intended to show how slum life made kids into criminals. Lillian Hellman did the screen adaptation of Sidney Kingsley's play, changing it as little as possible. Wyler, the natural choice for director, told Goldwyn that the movie should be made on location, in a real New York slum. Sam insisted that it was safer and wiser to work on a sound stage. The set Richard Day designed for the street—which included a stretch of the East River for the kids to swim in—was justly celebrated; its looming walls and narrow alleys invoked a claustrophobic feeling. Ultimately, though, Wyler had been right; the movie would have been done better on location. Its studio-bound look has dated a film that was remarkably original for its time.

The hero of *Dead End*, Joel McCrea, is a young man from the slums who has managed to become an architect. He is loved by a rich girl who lives in a mansion abutting the tenement section. In the end, he turns down the rich girl's offer to run away with him and marries another woman from the slum neighborhood, who is an activist for some unnamed social cause. The real thrust of the film is to examine the contrast of the rich people living on one side of the street and the poor people living *in* the street. Most of all, it is about a gang called the Dead End Kids. They play in the streets, swim in the dirty river, beat up a rich kid, and casually abuse and betray one another. Their lives are destined to be a dead end, like that of gangster Baby Face Martin, played by Humphrey Bogart, who returns to his old neighborhood and is finally shot down by the architect.

Above: *James Cagney starred with The Dead End Kids in* Angels with Dirty Faces *(1938).*

Right: *The Dead End Kids included (left to right, top) Billy Halop, Leo Gorcey, Gabriel Dell, Bernard Punsley, (bottom) Bobby Jordan (left), and Huntz Hall.*

Below right: *The setting for* Dead End *(1937) contrasted luxury apartments, complete with doorman, and the slum tenement next door.*

Though much of the film's story and atmosphere have been duplicated by dozens of later movies, *Dead End* still has impact. The atmosphere is unforgettable; one can almost smell the stale air and dirty river. All in all, it proved to be another solid addition to the list of Goldwyn classics. The movie did not succeed in giving the social message that it was meant to, however. The Dead End Kids, for example, had a long and surprising future in films. They went on to make sequels for other studios, including *Angels with Dirty Faces* (1938). Slowly, producers realized that these kids—among them Leo Gorcey, Huntz Hall, Bobby Jordan, and Gabe Dell—were not being perceived as the young hoodlums Kingsley had intended them to be. Instead, people tended to see them as a swell bunch of guys who never went to school and had a lot of fun. The Dead End Kids, renamed the Bowery Boys and various other names, ended up in a long series of low-budget comedies that lasted into the 1950s.

Dead End was nominated for the Best Picture Academy Award. This time Goldwyn was sure he would finally win it. The night of the award ceremony, he even had his acceptance speech prepared. However, the Best Picture Oscar of 1937 went to Warner's *The Life of Emile Zola*, as if fate were retaliating Goldwyn's mangling of Zola's *Nana*. (It is worth noting that this now-forgotten historical epic also won over a half-dozen other major or minor classics—*Captains Courageous, The Good Earth, In Old Chicago, Stage Door, A Star Is Born*, and *Lost Horizon*.)

That same year Goldwyn remade his old silent hit *Stella Dallas*. This time King Vidor was hired as director. Barbara Stanwyck played Stella. The audiences were not pleased. The public simply was tired of that kind of sob story. As one critic wrote, "I wept in 1925, but my eyes are dry today. I cannot believe Stella Dallas any more. She is too stupid for 1937." King Vidor was tired, too, of being run ragged by Goldwyn's demands during production. In the afternoon, Sam would be raging that everything was terrible; then in the middle of the night he would call Vidor to say everything was great. Vidor put a note on his desk that read, NO MORE GOLDWYN PICTURES, no matter how much Sam might offer him.

Another Goldwyn film of 1937 was *The Hurricane*, remembered today as mainly a "camp" classic and as the first appearance in a sarong of a lithe and exotic young lady named Dorothy Lamour. The story concerned the effect of a natural disaster in the South Seas. Typically, it was mostly shot on the Goldwyn lot, in this case by director John Ford.

One day Sam showed up on *The Hurricane* set to give some advice. As soon as he appeared, the set lapsed into an ominous silence. Ford, who was as tough as his pictures, growled, "You! Mr. Goldwyn! Whaddayawant?" Suddenly nervous, Sam suggested, very politely, that he would like more closeups. Ford demonstrated on Sam's body how he gauged closeups—with a smack to the stomach, the chest, and with his fist looming in front of Sam's face—and declared, "I'm making this picture the way *I* feel it should go." Shaken, Sam walked off, saying to an assistant, "Well anyway, I put it in his mind."

The Hurricane was a hit on its release. Though the director's work was admired, Ford himself hated the picture and would never work for Goldwyn again. Sam had driven away two fine directors, but he still had William Wyler.

Typically, a Goldwyn movie began with a story that happened to catch Sam's interest (often by way of Frances, who actually read books) and was then carefully developed into a script. Story conferences, always presided over by Sam personally, were usually frantic and nerve-wracking affairs, as writers and story editors tried to find the elusive something that would please their boss.

In 1938 Goldwyn had reclaimed Gary Cooper after the star's contract with Paramount had run out.

He immediately cast Cooper, for some incomprehensible reason, in the title role of *The Adventures of Marco Polo*. Cooper seemed uncomfortable in the part and the picture ended up, in Sam's own judgement, the worst flop of his entire career.

For Cooper's next film, Goldwyn decided to put his star safely into the expected cowboy role. Moreover, Sam wanted to co-star his then-favorite leading lady, Merle Oberon, a fine-featured beauty and a cool but sometimes effective actress, whose career had been in decline. The Cooper-Oberon vehicle was born in a famous (or rather, infamous) story conference at the studio. Director and one-time gag writer Leo McCarey lying on a couch, with his hands behind his head, spun an improbable, ideal story for Cooper and Oberon, using his comedic talents to put across a tale of a cowboy who is stuck in a little womanless town in Arizona and meets up with this elegant lady from a fancy girl's school in Virginia . . . and so on and so on. It was to be called *The Cowboy and the Lady*. The room rocked with laughter and amazement as McCarey's description of scenes and bits of action became wilder. Delighted, Sam left the meeting laughing. Next day, he bought the story from McCarey for $50,000.

The trouble was, there was no story. McCarey had been making it all up as he went and afterward couldn't remember a thing about it. He finally cooked up a short plot outline that, to say the least, did not earn his $50,000. Still, Sam had to have a picture for Cooper and Oberon. He hired the experienced team of Anita Loos and her husband John Emerson to write a script from the outline and offered McCarey the directing job. McCarey's astounding response: "What makes you think I would want to spend my valuable time on a piece of crap like *The Cowboy and the Lady*?"

The Cowboy and the Lady went through twenty-seven writers and three directors, actors switched roles in mid-production, expensive players like

David Niven vanished from the final cut, and the production ran over budget. Somehow, though, the final product was not entirely embarrassing, and at least it didn't lose money. All in all, *The Cowboy and the Lady* (1938), could have been much, much worse.

The same could be said of another production of that era which did smashing business at the box office—*The Goldwyn Follies* (1938), another of Sam's efforts to outdo Flo Ziegfeld in a variety show. For the movie, Sam simply brought together a variety of acts and actors that appealed to him, including ventriloquist Edgar Bergen, burlesque comedians the Ritz Brothers, elegant leading man Adolphe Menjou, and, for good measure, George Gershwin for the songs, and the entire Ballet of the Metropolitan Opera and its great choreographer George Balanchine for the dance sequences. The movie was intended to go from the sublime to the ridiculous, and it succeeded.

Laurence Olivier as Heathcliff and Geraldine Fitzgerald as his wife Isabella in Wuthering Heights *(1939).*

Sam had planned *The Goldwyn Follies* for years. In 1936, after turning down some quite good stories by eight or more writers, he settled on a script by Ben Hecht that lamely tried to tie together all the acts with some semblance of a plot. Meanwhile, fate cut short the brilliant career of George Gershwin; he completed only a few songs, including his last "Love Walked In," for the picture before dying of a brain tumor in 1937.

As *The New York Times* said after the premiere, *The Goldwyn Follies* has "a certain nightmarish quality," though the critic admitted, "Since it has the Goldwyn trademark, it goes without saying that it is a superior hodgepodge." In any case, the film was one of the big moneymakers of 1938.

On the heels of these lightweight movies came another classic that was both high-quality and, in the long run, very profitable—*Wuthering Heights* (1939), another William Wyler effort. The darkly romantic masterpiece by Emily Bronte had been a popular novel for almost a century. The novel had been con-

Merle Oberon starred as Cathy in Goldwyn's adaptation of Wuthering Heights.

sidered unfilmable, because it was a story that seemed to take place entirely in the characters' minds.

Charles MacArthur and Ben Hecht wrote a strong screenplay, based on the first half of the novel, for the producer Walter Wanger at United Artists. Wanger could not get the stars he wanted and sent the script across the lot to Wyler, who was thrilled with it and went to Goldwyn. Sam found it too sad, since the main characters die at the end. A few months later, though, Wyler convinced Sam to buy the screenplay by telling him that his competitor, Warner Bros., wanted the script, and moreover the leading role of Cathy was perfect for Merle Oberon. Sam immediately snapped it up. For the male lead, the tormented Heathcliff, Wyler turned to Laurence Olivier, a British stage actor who was unknown in the States and had been fired from his only previous American screen role as the hero in *Queen Christina*.

✳

*"Willie, if you
don't do
something about
this actor's ugly,
ugly, face, I stop
the picture!"*

Next, Wyler, who was as charming in everyday
life as he was brutal on the set, went after David
Niven to play Cathy's unfortunate husband Edgar.
Wyler promised Niven that he had changed and that
everything would be easy in this production. Taking
Wyler at his word, Niven signed a contract. On his
first day on the set, Niven found himself doing forty
takes of one scene for an increasingly nasty Wyler.

Exhausted, Niven finally shouted to the director, "You really are a son of a bitch, aren't you?"

"Yes," Wyler snarled, "and I'm going to be one
for fourteen weeks."

Olivier was also shaken by Wyler's Jekyll-and-
Hyde act, not to mention Sam Goldwyn's regular
explosions. Added to the personal conflicts was the
disaster of Olivier's boots. Olivier had been given a
nice pair of old leather boots from the costume
department, which looked as if they had been
tramping about the English moors for years. They
seemed just right for Heathcliff, but they also gave
Olivier a case of athlete's foot, which had become so
uncomfortable that for days he could hardly walk.
He tottered through the shooting in considerable
pain, somehow still giving a fine, sensitive performance.

Goldwyn was sympathetic, putting his arm
around Olivier and saying, "I've had it too, the same
trouble . . . That's no joke, that athletic feet." The
actor decided that Goldwyn was a pretty nice person, after all. The very next day, Sam stormed onto
the set in a rage and shouted to Wyler, "Wille, if you
don't do something about this actor's *ugly, ugly,* face,
I stop the picture!" Olivier was crushed. It finally
turned out that Sam was voicing mild concern about
some lighting effects that made Olivier's face look
dirty.

Niven ran into trouble again when he was sup-
posed to weep over the body of his dead wife. As
Merle Oberon lay obediently deceased, Niven nervously explained to Wyler that he didn't know how

to cry. Niven was ordered to lean over the prostrate Oberon and screw up his features while, off camera, someone blew menthol into his face to bring forth some tears.

Then, as Niven later recalled, "A terrible thing happened. Instead of tears coming out of my eyes, green slime came out of my nose."

" 'Ohhh! How *horrid!*' shrieked the corpse, who shot out of bed and disappeared at high speed into her dressing room."

There are obvious faults with *Wuthering Heights*. It is over-sentimental, Merle Oberon lacked the passion her part needed, and Sam's tacked-on ending of the dead lovers united in the heavens is downright silly. Still, the story of Cathy and her gypsy lover had been caught, however imperfectly, for eternity. For those who have seen the film, it has captured the feeling of the novel, and Olivier will always be Heathcliff. There have been remakes, but none as successful.

Once again, Goldwyn and Wyler received a row of Oscar nominations. *Wuthering Heights* was nominated for best picture, director, screenplay, music, actor, cinematography, and once again, the big awards eluded Sam. Only Gregg Toland won, for his superb camerawork. Nor was the film a major success on its first release, but it gained wide audiences in rerelease. Sam would always say that "Woodering Height," as he called it, was his favorite of all his films. (He would also say, "*I* made Woodering Height. Willie Wyler only directed it." This explains why Wyler would eventually leave to advance his career.)

Sam Goldwyn had achieved nearly everything he had wanted in his life and his career—money, respect, a family. But the biggest prize of all, the best-picture Oscar, seemed out of reach. It would finally come in the wake of war.

The Best Years
of His Life

*I*n 1940 the United States, though not actively at war with Germany and Japan, was preparing for that occurrence, and Sam Goldwyn was in conflict with United Artists. He and a partner had tried to buy that studio in 1937, for the company had long irritated him by making too many second-rate movies, which he felt lowered both his and the company's prestige. In the end, the irritation had degenerated into a battle of egos among Sam and the founders-owners of United Artists—D.W. Griffith, Mary Pickford, Charlie Chaplin, and Douglas Fairbanks, Sr.

The battle ended in 1941 when United Artists bought out Sam's interest and he moved to RKO for distribution. It was a blow for United Artists—Sam had made some 40 profitable movies in 15 years, a better record than any of the other United Artists-affiliated producers.

Opposite: *Babe Ruth (left) and Gary Cooper in* The Pride of the Yankees (1942).

Sam's first RKO release, in 1941, was a classic— *The Little Foxes*. In the making, though, it was to prove among the most painful of William Wyler's tenures on the set. Based on a play by Lillian Hellman, which she adapted for the screen, *The Little Foxes* concerned a vicious, scheming, post-Civil War family. For the part of Regina Giddings, a woman who defeats the businessmen around her by being more manipulating and merciless than they are, Wyler wanted Bette Davis. She was not only one of the screen's greatest actresses, but she was especially adept at playing strong-minded, often dominant, characters. By astute business and political manipulations, Goldwyn secured the loan of Bette Davis from Warner Bros., where she was under contract and for whom she was the top box-office draw. In return, Sam loaned Gary Cooper to Warner for the lead in *Sergeant York*.

Wyler had already directed Davis in two Warner Bros. films. For one of them, *Jezebel*, Davis won the second of her best-actress Oscars. (She claimed to have given the Academy Award its nickname when she noticed that the statuette's backside looked like her husband's; she started calling it by his middle name, which was Oscar.) Davis and Wyler had worked together at Warner, and they had a brief but passionate romance when her first marriage was falling apart.

Trouble started even before filming began. Wyler and Davis were both determined professionals, utterly devoted to their work, and right away they clashed over interpretation of the leading role. Wyler wanted Regina to be at first sympathetic and seductive, then to become cold and corrupt as greed mastered her. That way, Wyler felt, Regina's final outrage—refusing to bring her husband medicine and watching unmoved as he dies of a heart attack— would seem even more shocking. Davis was determined to take the opposite approach; Regina was to be a monster from the beginning, without feelings or a soul. To that end, Davis developed her own make-up —a cold, white, almost expressionless mask.

The filming of *The Little Foxes* was a nightmare, as the two, immovable in their opinions, engaged in an ascending series of clashes. Sam's incessant tinkering with Davis' costumes and hairstyle frayed her nerves even more. Finally, on the verge of a nervous breakdown after Wyler had attacked her approach once too often, Davis left the production for a week. During that week Wyler and Goldwyn considered signing up Davis' arch-rival, Miriam Hopkins, and reshooting the whole picture. But Davis returned and finished filming, compromising with Wyler enough to allow Regina a few flashes of mean-spirited humor.

Bette Davis hated her role and the picture. Amazingly, given the trials of its production, *The Little Foxes* turned out to be a masterful film. Held down to a few interior sets and stagey action, Wyler and Gregg Toland used all their artistry in visual expressiveness; every move of player and camera and editing was meaningful. And despite the unlovableness of most of the characters, this melodramatic tale of the corruption of a woman's feelings hit a strong nerve in the public and turned into box-office gold. It was another Goldwyn picture to be nominated for all the top Academy Awards, but to win none of them.

During World War II, Goldwyn entirely avoided the usual run of heroic war stories. His films that dealt most directly with combat were comedies, among them *They Got Me Covered* (1943), starring Bob Hope, and *Up In Arms* (1944), starring Goldwyn's discovery Danny Kaye.

The story of Kaye was a typical one. His first movie made him an "overnight" sensation only after he had worked his way painfully up the entertainment ladder for eleven years, starting as a clowning busboy in Catskill resorts and moving through nightclubs to Broadway. On the stage, his nimble-tongued patter songs, written by his wife Sylvia

The Kid from Brooklyn *(1946) starred Virginia Mayo and Danny Kaye— two Goldwyn discoveries.*

Fine, were a sensation. Goldwyn felt he could make this young comedian into another Eddie Cantor.

However, Kaye's first tests were disappointing; he looked like a blob on the screen. Sam took a good look, ordered Kaye's hair dyed blond and some discreet plastic surgery, and thus created the sharp-faced zany who would delight the world. *Up In Arms* was the first of a series of Technicolor Kaye comedies that were tremendously popular into the 1950s. Others included *Wonder Man* (1945), *The Secret Life of Walter Mitty* (1947), and *The Court Jester* (1955). *Wonder Man* was also the first starring film for Virginia Mayo, a Goldwyn actress of considerable beauty and limited acting range. Still, her beauty, somehow enhanced by a cast in one eye, gained her at least some theological importance: the Sultan of Morocco called Mayo "tangible proof for the existence of God."

Up In Arms also marked a significant Sam Goldwyn contribution to the future progress of the industry. Until the war, studios tended to be affiliated with syndicates that owned chains of theaters and booked films for the whole chain. Individual theaters were obliged to take what the syndicate gave them. The chain owners could dictate their own terms; this was especially hard on independent producers like Goldwyn.

Sam premiered *Up In Arms* in an independent theater in Chicago; then he wanted to mount a big opening in Reno, Nevada. When the syndicate that controlled the Reno chain offered him an unsatisfactory deal, Sam decided to buck the syndicate and show the film in a rented ballroom. The local police, no doubt encouraged by the syndicate, invoked regulations to stop the showing. Sam outwitted them by donating all the proceeds to the Red Cross and thus making the occasion a charity event. Sam and others went on to challenge the syndicates in court, and in 1946 the courts decreed an end to mass-bookings and the breaking up of the big theater chains. The result was a more flexible and competitive film industry—and bigger profits for Sam Goldwyn, who needed the money as his output declined to one or two movies a year. The major studios were then still making fifty or more features annually.

Another Goldwyn hit during the war was *The Pride of the Yankees* (1942), a biography of the triumphant career and tragic death of Lou Gehrig. Gehrig was played by Gary Cooper, who was certainly the image of an all-American ball player except for one problem—the British-educated Cooper had never played baseball in his life. Furthermore, he was right-handed and everybody knew that Gehrig had been a southpaw. The lanky actor tried to pass up the picture; he wanted instead to make *Reap the Wild Wind* for Cecil B. DeMille. Said Sam to his star, "Forget about raping the wind . . . The Gehrig thing is going to be a *great* picture."

The actor's inexperience required some very ingenious dodges in the filming. Doubles were used wherever possible: a double would slide into second in long-shot, Cooper would rise and dust himself off in close-up. He finally learned to hit a little, but threw the ball, observers noted, "like a girl." The problem of making Cooper seem left-handed required a more surrealistic solution. The whole ball-field was reversed, all player numbers and advertising signs were printed backwards, batters hit a single and sprinted for third base, and finally the film was flipped to turn everything back. All that on account of the star's right hand. It must have driven the real ball players on the set crazy.

The climax of the picture, when Gehrig says his farewell to Yankee fans because he is dying of a rare illness, amyotrophic lateral sclerosis (now called "Lou Gehrig's Disease"), was a re-creation of the real event. There was hardly a dry eye among viewers after Gehrig's noble conclusion, handled beautifully by Cooper, "I think I'm the luckiest guy on the face of the earth." Sam Goldwyn cried copiously over that performance, too. Cooper received a best-actor Oscar nomination for the role, only one year after winning it for *Sergeant York*. Quite appropriately, Danny Mandell collected an Academy Award for his editing, in which he managed to make Cooper look like a ball player.

Still another wartime, nonwar Goldwyn hit was a comedy called *Ball of Fire* (1944). Barbara Stanwyck played a sassy burlesque queen and gangster's girl who ended up under the protection of several professors who were writing an encyclopedia. Playing the unlikely role of an absent-minded intellectual, Gary Cooper was delightful; his "aw shucks" shyness made the part both believable and funny. Cooper enjoyed the picture, though he demanded that Sam tone down some of the pseudo-scholarly gibberish in Billy Wilder's script: "Two-dollar words, okay," said Cooper, "but not *ten*-dollar words."

The one Goldwyn film of the war years that tried to deal seriously with the conflict was unconventional, and bitterly controversial. This was *The North Star* (1943), which described life in a Russian village devastated by the Nazis. The uproar this film caused was largely the result of an ideological conflict. The Soviet Union and its leader Stalin were perceived in the United States as evil and dangerous. However, Russia *was* an ally, fighting against Hitler and Germany, and in fact was doing most of the fighting and dying. The point of Lillian Hellman's screenplay for *The North Star* was to emphasize the second point and to gain some sympathy for an ally by showing the suffering caused by the Nazi invasion of Russia. The basic idea had been suggested by President Roosevelt personally.

Lewis Milestone, director of the classic war film *All Quiet on the Western Front* (1930), signed on for *The North Star* knowing full well that it was Goldwyn's tendency to, as Milestone put it, "eat directors for breakfast." Sam lived up to Milestone's expectations. The director didn't hit it off with Lillian Hellman, either. Both resisted all Milestone's suggestions about the story. Art director William Cameron Menzies, who had designed *Gone with the Wind* (1939), tried to equal that spectacle in *The North Star*. He built a ten-acre Russian village on the studio back lot, authentic down to the cows. At the end of the picture the whole village was torched as the people fled the Nazis. The star was a very young and handsome Goldwyn discovery named Farley Granger.

On release the picture proved to be a disappointment. Despite all the research to make the settings and costumes authentic, the Russian peasants were portrayed as a rather charming collection of small-town Americans. That disturbed some critics. At the same time, the very fact that Russians were presented sympathetically outraged the American right wing. Newspapers branded the film "pure Bolshevist propaganda" and called Lillian Hellman "a partisan pleader for Communist causes." Incredibly, some even accused *The North Star* of being Nazi propaganda. Despite some good reviews—punning on the director's name, *Time* called it a "cinemilestone"—the picture never made back its price tag of two-million dollars. Later, renamed *Armored Attack*, it was among the first of his movies that Goldwyn sold off to television. The new version removed all possible references to Russia, making it seem to take place in no specific country.

Having avoided the usual type of war pictures, Goldwyn then came up with an idea that led to one of the greatest films ever made about the end of a war. In 1945 Sam and Frances were reading *Time* magazine and noticed an article and pictures about injured servicemen and the postwar problems they faced at home. Maybe, Sam thought, there was a movie in that.

Sam asked novelist and war correspondent McKinlay Kantor for a story on the subject. Kantor wrote a novel called *Glory for Me,* which was done entirely in blank verse—an indication of the poetic

The Best Years of His Life

Harold Russell, a real life ex-sailor who never acted professionally before, is one of the three main characters in The Best Years of Our Lives. *He won the Oscar for best supporting actor.*

quality of his story, which would ultimately have its effect on the film.

Next, Sam asked one of his favorite screenwriters, Robert E. Sherwood, to turn Kantor's novel into a screenplay. By then, William Wyler had returned from making films for the army and also became involved. From the beginning, there was something special about this project. It was done mainly by men who had been to war and had profound feelings about it. Sensing that, Sam uncharacteristically told Wyler and Sherwood, "I don't want you to think of this as a Hollywood picture. I want something simple and believable."

The result turned out very much that way: simple on the surface, intensely real, and rather unlike Hollywood. Its final title, *The Best Years of Our Lives*, was picked from a list of titles by preview audiences. In the film, three men returned from the war—a bombadier, an infantry sergeant, and a sailor who had lost his hands and now used mechanical hooks. The bombadier was played by Dana Andrews, the sergeant by Fredric March, and the sailor by a nonprofessional, an ex-sailor named Harold Russell, whose hands were indeed missing. Myrna Loy, a major star noted for glamorous and sophisticated parts, signed on to play a supporting role as March's wife; Teresa Wright played their daughter.

Time has dimmed the impact and originality of many of Samuel Goldwyn's best pictures, such as

In The Best Years of Our Lives *(1946) Teresa Wright tells her parents, played by Myrna Loy and Fredric March, that she is in love with a married man.*

Dana Andrews plays an Air Force veteran in The Best Years of Our Lives. *Here, in a famous scene, he relives some of his wartime experiences.*

Dead End and *The Little Foxes*, but that is not the case with *The Best Years of Our Lives*. It remains one of the most moving, timeless, and unconventional studio films Hollywood ever made.

There are no action scenes, no glamor, virtually no plot. Things happen apparently aimlessly, as they do in real life, And yet the film—unusually long at two and one-half hours—flows forward without a halt, always fascinating to watch. The three men, having been forever changed by war, try to pick up their lives. The bombadier discovers that his war bride is an empty-headed showgirl and that they no longer know each other, if they ever did. Soon he finds himself once again working in the drugstore from which he had escaped by going to war. The sergeant discovers his children are suddenly and bewilderingly grown. The handicapped sailor can hardly bear the pity of his family or of his fiancée. Everyone in the film stumbles on, trying to find some way back into normal life but not knowing how.

One remembers *The Best Years of Our Lives* not as a story but as a collage of memorable moments, covering a wide spectrum of emotions in the lives of people for whom we deeply care. A father wordlessly helps his maimed son get ready for bed. The sailor, mistakenly thinking that kids outside are making fun of him, drives his hooks through a window (a shocking moment in this gentle film). A young girl fearlessly tells her father that she loves a married man. The sergeant, drunk again, is shepherded by his wife and daughter with amusement, love, and concern. The bombadier sits lost in thought in the plexiglass nose of a junked bomber in an airplane graveyard. In the end the sailor marries his girl, the flier leaves his wife and finds a new one, the sergeant returns to his bank; but nothing is neatly resolved or settled, just as things in real life are never really settled.

Wyler was at the peak of his art in this film, handling an intimate human drama with absolute mastery; he had found a subject and an approach that suited him perfectly. Gregg Toland's deep-focus photography had never been more poetically used to help create a many layered emotional experience.

The Best Years of Our Lives was an instant success, not only in the United States but also in Great Britain. And this time, Sam Goldwyn finally won his Oscars—seven of them: Best Picture, Best Direction, Best Screenplay, Best Actor (Fredric March), Best Supporting Actor (the amateur Harold Russell), Best Editing, and Best Musical Score. Moreoever, Sam was presented the highest accolade a producer can receive, the Irving Thalberg Award: "In recognition of a constant high quality of motion picture production," the citation said. A tearful Sam posed awkwardly, but proudly, for the cameras, his first Oscar in one hand and the Thalberg trophy in the other.

Soon after, Sam took Frances on a trip to Gloversville, New York, the scene of his first years in America. They returned to the old glove factory and the hotel where the drummers first seized his imagination with a vision of success in the great world. Sam wanted to see once more, and to show his wife and partner, the place where he began his climb. Now he had reached the top of the mountain.

Chapter 12

The Final Reel

When Sam achieved his goal, with *The Best Years of Our Lives*, he was sixty-five years old, nearing the end of his own best years. His wife Frances said of the weeks after the Oscars that he looked like "a child who'd gotten everything he wanted for Christmas." But already he was beginning to wonder if there was nowhere to go but down. That would prove to be true.

The decline began when director William Wyler departed. Wyler's ten years with Goldwyn had been the longest and most fruitful collaboration of either man's life. With the money his biggest film brought in, Wyler simply decided he did not have to put up with Sam Goldwyn anymore. In the long career that ensued, which included winning multiple Oscars for *Ben Hur* in 1959, Wyler would never quite reach the heights he did in his Goldwyn years.

Another major element of the "Goldwyn touch" was lost in 1948, when Gregg Toland suddenly died of a heart attack at age forty-four. Never again would a Goldwyn film have the atmosphere and poetic expressiveness that only Toland's camera could create. In an interview just before he died, Toland said of his boss: "Goldwyn will allow me more freedom, more experiments, and more ideas than anyone . . . I believe he tries harder than any other person in the industry. He isn't always right, but he *tries*." When Sam was told of Toland's death, he dissolved in tears. He knew better than anyone else just how dedicated his cameraman was, and what the screen had lost.

Goldwyn's personal intensity never slacked. He still tried; he still drove his employees hard. Somehow, though, the magic had slipped away from his grasp. The end of the 1940s saw more Danny Kaye comedies, including the most popular of all, *The Secret Life of Walter Mitty* (1947). Though based on James Thurber's immortal short story of a mild man who dreams of adventure, the story became a frame for Kaye's comedy routines, which did not hurt the movie's profits but did hurt its quality. Thurber himself was outraged with the results.

Another Kaye film (like *Mitty*, co-starring Virginia Mayo) was *A Song Is Born* (1946), a remake of *Ball of Fire*. This version also was directed by Howard Hawks. The film featured several musical stars including Louis Armstrong, Benny Goodman, Lionel Hampton, and Tommy Dorsey. Despite the best efforts of all this talent, the film fell flat. Part of the problem was Sam's differences with Kaye's wife, Sylvia Fine, a songwriter. As a result, there were no songs performed by Kaye—and audiences came mainly to hear him sing.

The Bishop's Wife (1946) was more of a success, although it did not live up to its talent—screenwriter Robert E. Sherwood and stars Cary Grant, Loretta Young, David Niven, and Elsa Lanchester. The comedy concerns an angel who is sent from heaven to call a bishop back to his wife and congregation when the bishop has become obsessed with building a cathedral. The production fell into chaos, during which one director was fired and the second started again from scratch; the leading lady was replaced; and Sam reversed the roles of Niven and Grant in mid-production (Grant felt very uncomfortable in his final role as the angel, but received an Oscar nomination for the part). When production resumed under director Henry Koster, it was discovered that Grant and Loretta Young both refused to be photographed on the right side of their faces, which they were convinced looked weak. The outcome was that they could not be photographed talking face-to-face. (Sam solved that problem by threatening to pay Young half a salary for half her face; she then became more agreeable.) The resulting picture was reasonably funny and profitable, but it was not up to the old Goldwyn standard.

❋

In one of his finest moments, Sam Goldwyn stood up to HUAC.

Another postwar circumstance affected all of Hollywood, not just Sam Goldwyn. In 1947 a wave of anti-Communist hysteria broke out across the country, emanating mainly from the Congressional House Un-American Activities Committee (HUAC). The committee's first big target was the Hollywood artists who leaned to the political left. After testimony from witnesses denouncing their colleagues (these witnesses included Adolphe Menjou, Robert Montgomery, Ronald Reagan, and Walt Disney), ten writers were indicted and eventually imprisoned. Over the next few years, there was a nationwide witch hunt to sniff out suspected Communists. In Hollywood the careers of some of the best people in the industry came to an abrupt end, and the creative freedom of movies generally suffered.

In one of his finest moments, Sam Goldwyn stood up to HUAC. He hated Russia and Communism as much as anybody, but what he saw happening in America reminded him of the Russian anti-Semitic rampages of his youth. He could not see how it squared with American ideals, for the government to take away an artist's right to work.

In the 1950s the House Un-American Activities Committee investigated the Hollywood community for communist influences. Here John Garfield, famous movie 'tough guy,' testifies in 1951.

When Sam learned that HUAC was planning to call up screenwriter Robert E. Sherwood to question him about some of his supposedly leftist scenes in *The Best Years of Our Lives,* Sam was furious. It was clear that, had this kind of repression been active two years earlier, *The Best Years* could not even have been made. Sam wrote a letter to the committee supporting his writer and demanded to testify himself. HUAC then quietly dropped the investigation of Sherwood. But Sam could do little about the fear that ruled Hollywood into the 1950s, or the persecutions that ruined dozens of film artists, most of them entirely guiltless. (As in Stalin's Russia, artistic criticism of such repression had to be expressed obliquely, in comedy or between the lines of drama. One example is the thriller *Invasion of the Body Snatchers* (1956), in which decent citizens are replaced by unthinking, conforming duplicates.)

The "Goldwyn touch" lost its luster in the films of the late 1940s and early 1950s. Sam made some middling-to-unsuccessful films featuring Farley Granger and Dana Andrews, both of whose careers floundered as a result. *I Want You* (1951), for example, starring Granger and Andrews was a pale attempt at another *The Best Years*, in the context of the Korean War. Goldwyn had made plenty of failures in his career—ones that failed in quality but succeeded at the box office, ones that did the reverse, and ones that failed on all fronts—but he had always managed to compensate with a commercial and/or critical blockbuster. Now there were no more blockbusters.

The old Hollywood was falling apart, torn by the witch hunt and by the competition of the new medium of television. Rather than going out to the movies once or twice a week as a matter of habit, many people stayed at home and watched television. Hollywood tried to draw back the public with new techniques like wide-screen and 3-D pictures; results were modest at best. In 1945, approximately 90,000,000 Americans a week went to the movies and 350 films were released. With a much larger population in 1967, less than 18,000,000 attended the movies weekly and 178 films were released. (In the mid-1980s, more than 22,500,000 people went to the movies each week, but even fewer new American films were released).

It seems that many great men are praised and rewarded as they get to the end of a career. Sam was profiled in *Life* magazine; his charitable contributions were lauded by the United Jewish Appeal; Beverly Hills mounted a "Samuel Goldwyn Day." As always, dignitaries visiting in Hollywood stopped at Sam's house for dinner; Sam considered Winston Churchill and other world leaders to be his personal friends. In decline, he still commanded the power of his name and personality.

Sam Goldwyn on the set of Porgy and Bess *in 1958.*

His pictures dwindled to fewer than one a year. The last three, dated 1952, 1955, and 1959, form a descending series. Danny Kaye starred in *Hans Christian Andersen* (1952), a fictionalized account of the Danish storyteller who created "The Ugly Duckling" and other fairy tales. It was lambasted by the critics but did good business, mainly due to several hit Frank Loesser songs, including "Wonderful Copenhagen." The musical *Guys and Dolls* (1956) cast Marlon Brando and Frank Sinatra in the unlikely roles of singing gangsters, and was Frances Goldwyn's pet project. This film also was uneven and critically booed, but publicity and Frank Loesser's score brought in the audiences.

Finally came the calamitous *Porgy and Bess* (1959). Sam paid three-quarters of a million dollars for the rights to George Gershwin's folk opera about poor Southern blacks on "Catfish Row" in Charleston, South Carolina. The songs alone seemed to make it worth the price; they include "Summertime," "Bess, You Is My Woman Now," and "It Ain't Necessarily So." In 1957 Sam announced that he had signed black star Sidney Poitier to play Porgy.

Times had changed from the years when the opera was considered to be a story about the real lives of black people. In a climate of increasing militancy and tension over civil rights, black leaders saw it as a demeaning white distortion of black society. Sam never understood this reaction, but Poitier was quick to feel and understand the pressure; the star withdrew, but Sam coaxed him back. Finally, other top black performers signed on, among them Dorothy Dandridge, Sammy Davis, Jr., and Pearl Bailey.

It took six months to build the gigantic set of Catfish Row on a Goldwyn sound stage. In the summer of 1957, the set, costumes, props, and sound stage all went up in flames; somebody had left a burning cigarette on a mattress. Doggedly, Goldwyn decreed that everything be rebuilt. As that was being done, he fired director Rouben Mamoulian after a bitter series of disagreements. Mamoulian lodged a formal complaint that led, temporarily, to a Screen Actors Guild boycott on Goldwyn. Finally, Goldwyn hired director Otto Preminger, who had less talent than Mamoulian but even more ego. At one point, Sam tried to fire Preminger, too, but the director refused to leave.

Not surprisingly, by this time everyone was beginning to regard *Porgy and Bess* as a cursed production. It was finished amidst attacks from civil

Pearl Bailey and Sidney Poitier in Porgy and Bess *(1959). This was Samuel Goldwyn's last film.*

rights organizations, cast objections to the low-life aspects of the script, and ear-splitting arguments between director and producer. Despite some good singing from the cast and Oscar-winning musical arrangements, the film was panned by the press ("a patronizing caricature of Negro life") and shunned by the public.

When *Porgy and Bess* was released in 1959, Sam Goldwyn was seventy-seven years old, a relic of a vanishing Hollywood and its legendary moguls. He, Jesse Lasky, Adolph Zukor, and Jack Warner had been the founders of the industry. Now young American-born businessmen were taking over. Over the years Sam continued to plan and peddle dozens of stories, but nothing quite took shape. He visited his office, but the Goldwyn lot was eerily quiet and empty. In 1969 he suffered the first of several strokes. Confined to a wheelchair, Sam Goldwyn gradually settled into a smiling sleep. He died that way, at ninety-one, in January 1974.

Sam Goldwyn was responsible for a handful of Hollywood's finest films, and for dozens of lesser movies that still delight and move millions of people around the world. The word *responsible* is used deliberately: Sam did not, as he tried to claim, actually make the movies; his employees did. But he originated them and stamped them with his passion for quality and a sincere desire to avoid the obvious and the hackneyed. He was not an artist, exactly, but many artists did their best work for him, and he had the instincts to know something good when he saw it. His quarreling and childishness were certainly not admirable; but Goldwyn felt personal responsibility for each film, and was willing to fight for his beliefs, as well as pay gigantic sums out of his own pocket. That alone would have killed most people. Sam Goldwyn seemed to revel in the situation, but it could hardly improve his personality.

Sam Goldwyn was an immigrant who started with nothing and raised himself entirely by his labor to become one of the most prominent men in the world. He wanted to become rich and famous and he did. He wanted to maintain a high standard as well, and often as not he did that too. As Gregg Toland said, "He is not always right, but he *tries*."

In driving for both broad entertainment and high quality, he tended to hit somewhere between those two goals: other producers made more money than he did (Sam left an estate of four-million dollars, a handsome sum but far from the wealth of many Hollywood stars), and some producers maintained a higher standard of quality. Of all Goldwyn films, only *The Best Years of Our Lives* is mentioned as one of the ten all-time screen masterpieces.

In his life and in his work, Sam Goldwyn showed us something profound about success, that discerning it is often like panning a stream: one has to look hard amidst the mud to find the shining bits of gold.

Bibliography

Agee, James. *Agee on Film*. New York: G. P. Putnam's Sons, 1958.

Brownlow, Kevin. *The Parade's Gone By*. New York: Alfred A. Knopf, 1969.

Essoe, Gabe and Raymond Lee. *DeMille, The Man and His Pictures*. New York: A.S. Barnes & Co., Inc., 1970.

Goldwyn, Samuel. *Behind the Screen*. New York: George H. Doran, 1923.

Jacobs, Lewis. *The Rise of the American Film*. New York: W.W. Norton, 1968.

Johnson, Alma. *The Great Goldwyn*. New York: Random House, 1937.

Kanin, Garson. *Hollywood*. New York: Viking, 1974.

Katz, Ephraim. *The Film Encyclopedia*. New York: T.Y. Crowell, 1979.

Lyon, Christopher, ed. *The International Dictionary of Films and Filmmakers*. New York: The Putnam Publishing Group, 1985.

Marx, Arthur. *Goldwyn: A Biography of the Man Behind the Myth*. New York: W.W. Norton, 1976.

Mast, Gerald. *A Short History of the Movies*. Indianapolis: The Bobbs-Merrill Co., Inc., 1971.

May, Lary. *Screening Out the Past: The Birth of Mass Culture and the Motion Picture Industry*. New York: Oxford University Press, 1980.

Niven, David. *The Moon's a Balloon*. New York: G. P. Putnam's Sons, 1972.

Ramsaye, Terry. *A Million and One Nights*. New York: Simon & Schuster, Inc., 1926.

Robinson, David, ed. *Movies of the Forties*. London: Orbis Publishing, 1982.

Rosenberg, Bernard and Harry Silverstein. *The Real Tinsel*. New York: Macmillan, 1970.

Shipman, David. *The Story of Cinema*. New York: St. Martin's Press, 1982.

Index

U

V

W

Y

Z

Acknowledgments and Credits

Frontispiece and pages 6, 10, 14, 32, 64, 82, and 119, Culver Pictures, Inc.

Pages 18, 19, 24, 28–29, 41, 54, 55, 59, 62, 72, 78, 80, 96, 100, 101, 104, 108, 112 bottom, and 121, Jerry Vermilye.

Page 36; The Performing Arts Research Center, New York Public Library at Lincoln Center.

Pages 44, 45, 50, 112 top, and 113, Photofest.

Page 66, The California Historical Society, Los Angeles History Center Photographic Collections.

Page 118, Associated Press.

14728

92
Go

Barnes, Jeremy

Samuel Goldwyn

DATE DUE	BORROWER	
DEC 1	Dan Kirley 8A 104	

14728

92
Go

Barnes, Jeremy

Samuel Goldwyn

Library Media Center
Madison Central School
Madison, N.Y., 13402

 GUMDROP BOOKS - Bethany, Missouri